I0435128

# Forecasts of County-Level Land Uses Under Three Future Scenarios

### A Technical Document Supporting the Forest Service 2010 RPA Assessment

## David N. Wear

**The Author:**

**David N. Wear**, Research Forester and Project Leader, Forest Economics and Policy Work Unit, U.S. Forest Service, Southern Research Station, Forestry Sciences Laboratory, 3041 Cornwallis Rd., Research Triangle Park, NC 27713.

**Product Disclaimer**

The use of trade or firm names in this publication is for reader information and does not imply endorsement by the U.S. Department of Agriculture of any product or service.

August 2011

Southern Research Station
200 W. T. Weaver Blvd.
Asheville, NC 28804

# Forecasts of County-Level Land Uses Under Three Future Scenarios: A Technical Document Supporting the Forest Service 2010 RPA Assessment

David N. Wear

# CONTENTS

Page

# LIST OF TABLES

# LIST OF FIGURES

# Forecasts of County-Level Land Uses Under Three Future Scenarios: A Technical Document Supporting the Forest Service 2010 RPA Assessment

David N. Wear

## Abstract

Accurately forecasting future forest conditions and the implications for ecosystem services depends on understanding land use dynamics. In support of the 2010 Renewable Resources Planning Act (RPA) Assessment, we forecast changes in land uses for the coterminous United States in response to three scenarios. Our land use models forecast urbanization in response to the population and economic projections defined by the scenarios and consequences for various rural land uses. Urban area is forecasted to expand by 1 to 1.4 million acres per year between 1997 and 2060. Forest area is forecasted to decline by 24 to 37 million acres and cropland is forecasted to decline by 19 to 28 million acres over this period. About 90 percent of forecasted forest land losses are found in the Eastern United States with more than half in the South.

Keywords: Assessments, forecasting, land use.

## INTRODUCTION

The Forest and Rangeland Renewable Resources Planning Act (RPA) of 1974 mandates a periodic assessment of the condition and trends of the Nation's renewable resources. The 2010 RPA Assessment provides a snapshot of current U.S. forest and rangeland conditions and trends on all ownerships, identifies drivers of change, and projects 50 years into the future. Analyses of the status and trends for recreation, water, timber, wildlife (biodiversity) and range resources as well as land-use change, climate change, and urban forestry are included (USDA Forest Service 2001).

Because land use patterns define the template upon which natural systems develop and affects the flow of all ecosystem services, forecasts of land use changes are a key element of the RPA Assessment. Forecasts of forest and nonforest uses are important inputs into analysis of forest conditions, wildlife habitat, carbon storage, and water demands, among others. This paper presents the land use forecasts associated with the three scenarios that frame the 2010 RPA Assessment.

## FORECASTING APPROACH

We forecast land use distributions at the county level for all counties in the coterminous United States using econometric models fit to historical data (Wear 2010). Separate models were estimated for each of four assessment regions (South, North, Rockies, and Pacific) with two exceptions. Texas and Oklahoma were split between regions, with the forested eastern portions of each State included in the South's model and the remainder in the Rockies' model. For model estimation then, Texas and Oklahoma counties were included with regions with most similar conditions, but for all reporting we aggregate all of Texas and Oklahoma into the South, consistent with the Forest Service Assessment Regions shown in figure 1.

Our land use models have two major components. In the first component, changes in county-level population and personal income are used to simulate future urbanization. The second component allocates rural land among competing uses. The econometric models developed by Wear (2010) were fit to land use change data from 1987 and 1997 to ensure that forecasted land use changes are generally consistent with observed urbanization intensities and rural land use changes. For the forecasts developed here, we hold constant the real rents of both agricultural and forest land uses—in effect assuming that the relative returns to these uses remains constant through the forecast period. We also examine where substitution between rural land uses might be concentrated in the United States under futures that alter the relative returns to forestry and agriculture. Details regarding the modeling approach are contained in Appendices A and B.

Observations of historical land uses were derived from the National Resource Inventory (NRI) survey of land uses conducted for the years 1987 and 1997. The NRI provides the only consistent, repeated, and exhaustive measure of non-Federal land uses in the United States, and 1997 is the last year for which detailed data are currently available. We

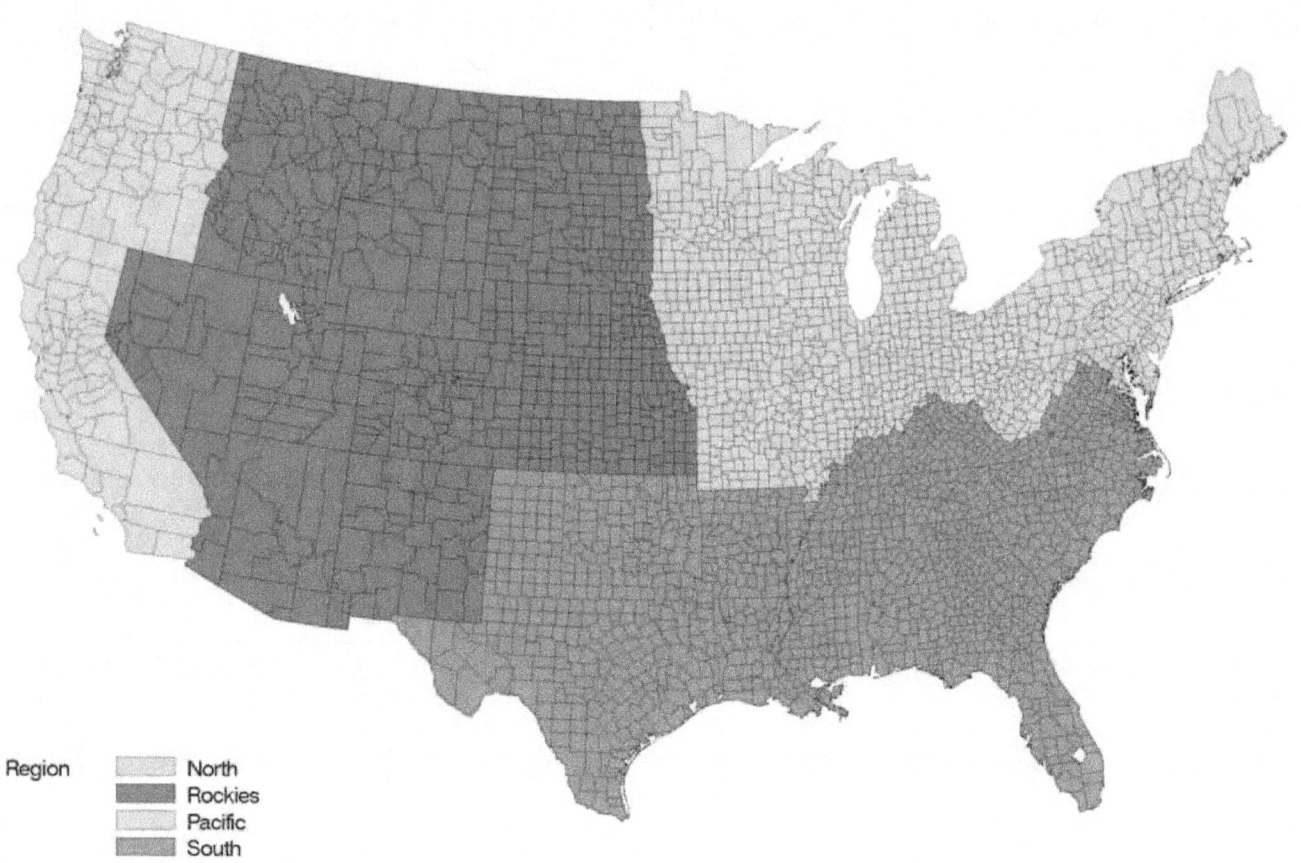

Figure 1—Definition of the RPA Assessment Regions.

Region
- North
- Rockies
- Pacific
- South

used NRI county estimates of the areas of non-Federal land in pasture, cropland, forest, range, or urban uses (see table 1), and define this as the total "mutable" land. All modeled land use change is within this land base; other land uses, including federal land, water area, enrolled Conservation Reserve Program lands, and utility corridors are held constant for all forecasts.

The distributions of the five modeled land uses for non-Federal land in 1997 are shown in the five panels of figure 2. Patterns of rural uses reflect biome boundaries (e.g., natural boundaries between grassland and forest land) and productivity determined by biophysical conditions along with comparative advantages for producing various goods and services determined by cost and return attributes. Forest uses dominate the South, the Northeast, the Lake States, and the Pacific Northwest. Cropland is concentrated in the Plains and Midwest, while rangeland is concentrated in the High Plains and intermountain West. Urban land, the least abundant land use, corresponds with the Nation's cities, and the largest area of pastureland is found at the boundary between grassland and forest biomes from eastern Texas to northern Missouri.

Each of the four assessment regions has a distinctive distribution of non-Federal land uses (fig. 3). The Rockies is dominated by rangeland, while the South has the largest concentration of forests among regions. The North has the largest share of cropland, roughly equivalent to the area of forest land in the North.

**Table 1—Definitions of land use categories in the NRI***

**Forest land:**
A land cover/use category that is at least 10 percent stocked by single stemmed forest trees of any size which will be at least 4 m (13 feet) tall at maturity. When viewed vertically, canopy cover is 25 percent or greater. Also included are areas bearing evidence of natural regeneration of tree cover (cutover forest or abandoned farmland) and not currently developed for nonforest use. For classification as forest land, an area must be at least 1 acre and 100 feet wide.

**Cropland:**
A land cover/use category that includes areas used for the production of adapted crops for harvest. Two subcategories of cropland are recognized: cultivated and noncultivated. Cultivated cropland comprises land in row crops or close-grown crops and also other cultivated cropland, for example, hayland or pastureland that is in a rotation with row or close-grown crops. Noncultivated cropland includes permanent hayland and horticultural cropland.

**Rangeland:**
A land cover/use category on which the climax or potential plant cover is composed principally of native grasses, grasslike plants, forbs or shrubs suitable for grazing and browsing, and introduced forage species that are managed like rangeland. This would include areas where introduced hardy and persistent grasses, such as crested wheatgrass, are planted and such practices as deferred grazing, burning, chaining, and rotational grazing are used, with little or no chemicals or fertilizer being applied. Grasslands, savannas, many wetlands, some deserts, and tundra are considered to be rangeland. Certain communities of low forbs and shrubs, such as mesquite, chaparral, mountain shrub, and pinyon-juniper, are also included as rangeland.

**Urban and built-up areas:**
A land cover/use category consisting of residential, industrial, commercial, and institutional land; construction sites; public administrative sites; railroad yards; cemeteries; airports; golf courses; sanitary landfills; sewage treatment plants; water control structures and spillways; other land used for such purposes; small parks (< 10 acres) within urban and built-up areas; and highways, railroads, and other transportation facilities if they are surrounded by urban areas. Also included are tracts of < 10 acres that do not meet the above definition but are completely surrounded by Urban and Built-up land. Two size categories are recognized in the NRI: (1) areas 0.25 to 10 acres, and (2) areas > 10 acres.

**Pastureland and Native Pasture:**
A land cover/use category of land managed primarily for the production of introduced or native forage plants for livestock grazing. Pastureland may consist of a single species in a pure stand, a grass mixture or a grass-legume mixture. Management usually consists of cultural treatments—fertilization, weed control, reseeding, or renovation and control of grazing. (For the NRI, includes land that has a vegetative cover of grasses, legumes, and/or forbs, regardless of whether or not it is being grazed by livestock.)

*NRI = Natural Resource Inventory.

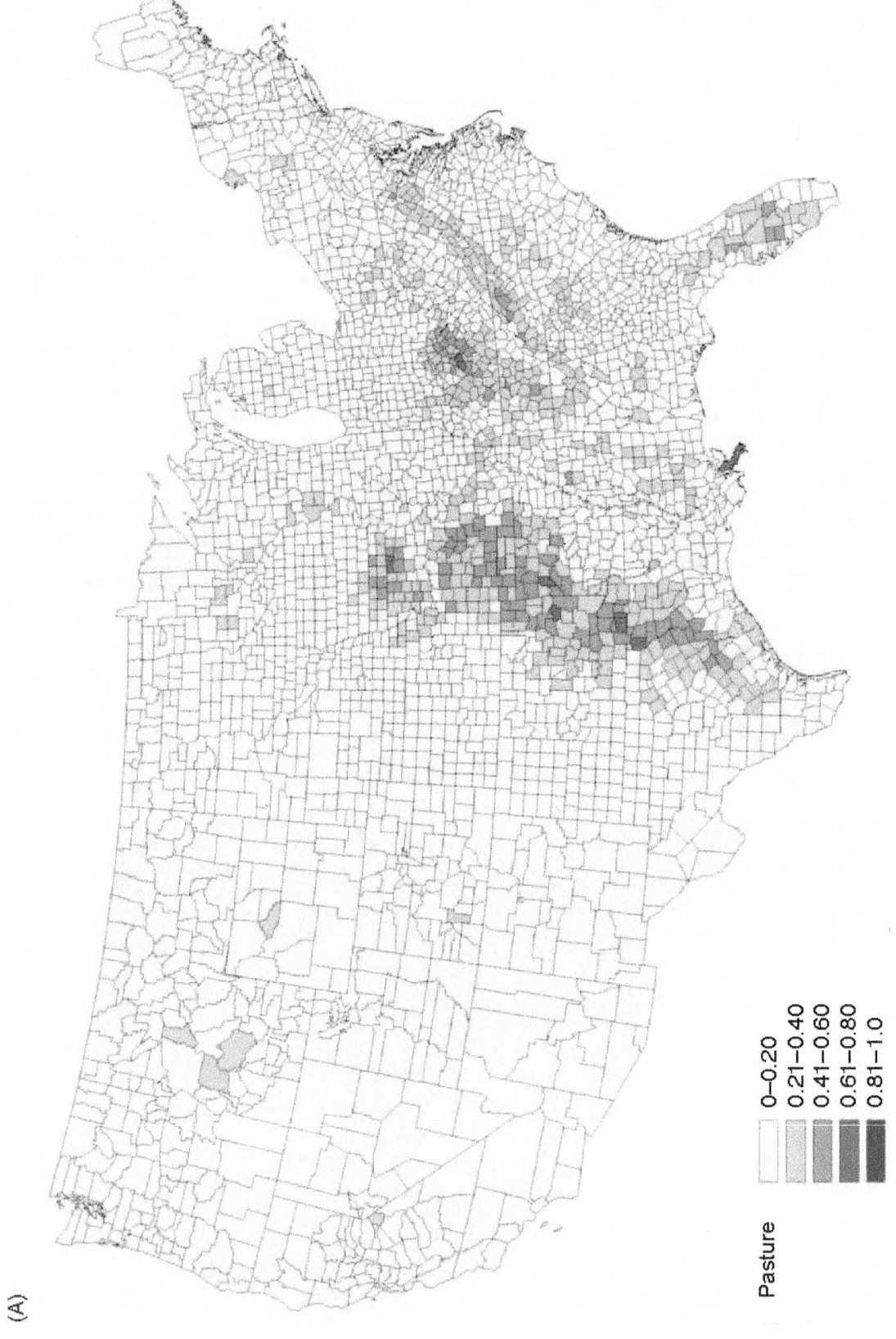

Pasture

0–0.20
0.21–0.40
0.41–0.60
0.61–0.80
0.81–1.0

(A)

Figure 2—Concentration of five land uses (proportion of each county) on nonfederal land, 1997: (A) pasture, (B) crops, (C) forest, (D) range, (E) urban. (Source: NRI) (continued to next page)

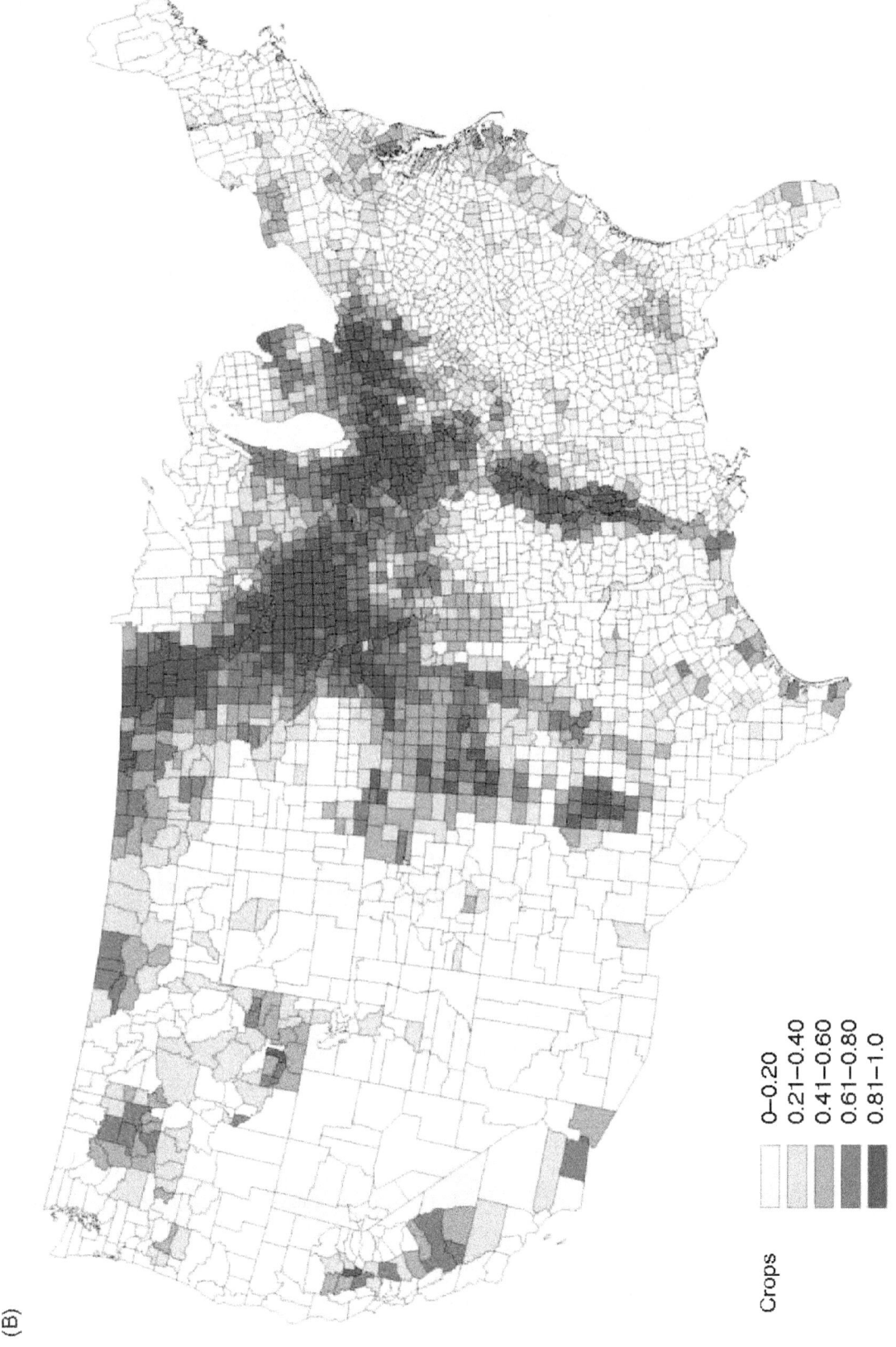

(B)

Crops

0–0.20
0.21–0.40
0.41–0.60
0.61–0.80
0.81–1.0

Figure 2 (continued)—Concentration of five land uses (proportion of each county) on nonfederal land, 1997: (A) pasture, (B) crops, (C) forest, (D) range, (E) urban. (Source: NRI) (continued to next page)

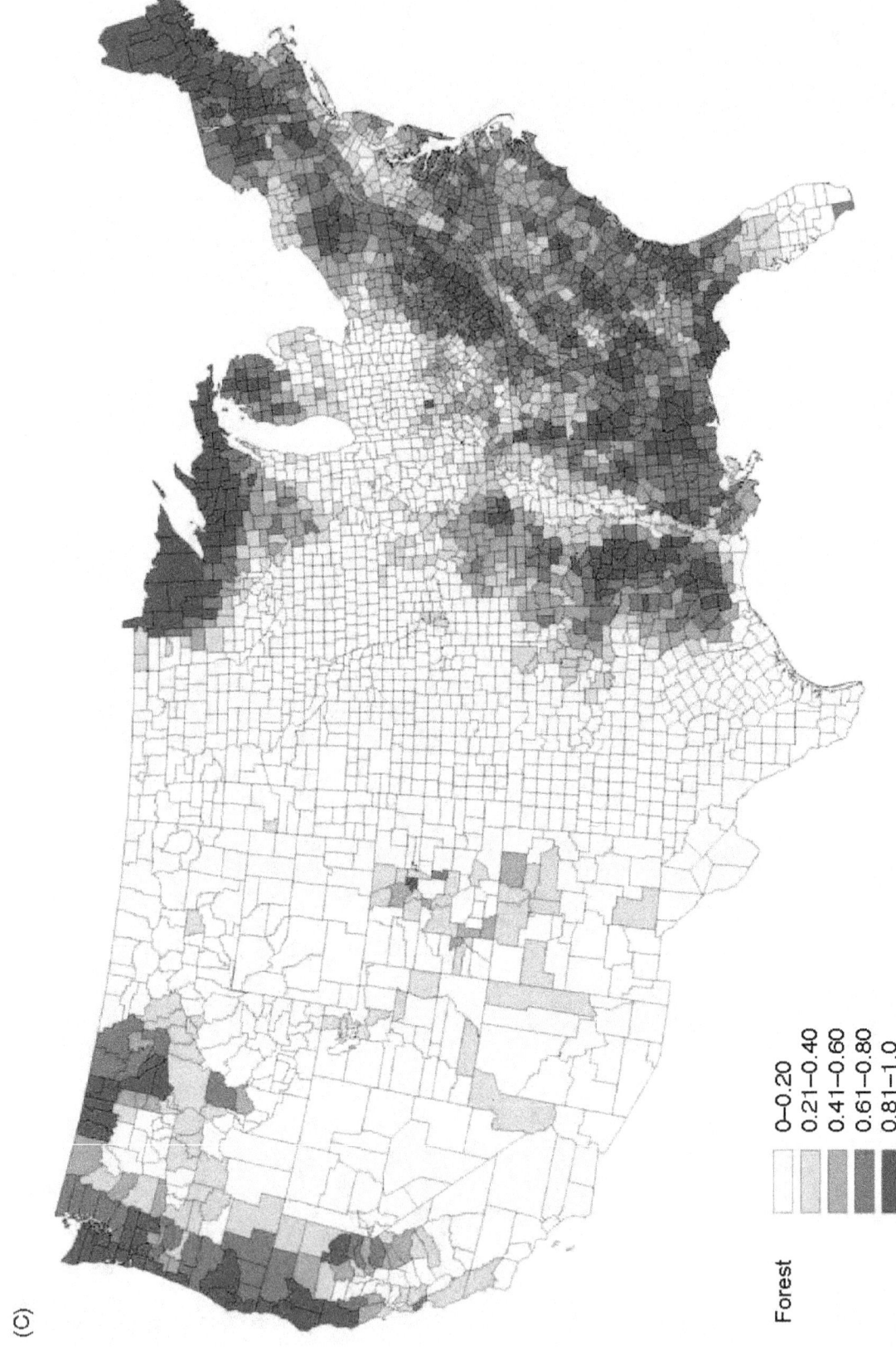

(C)

Forest

0–0.20
0.21–0.40
0.41–0.60
0.61–0.80
0.81–1.0

Figure 2 (continued)—Concentration of five land uses (proportion of each county) on nonfederal land, 1997. (A) pasture, (B) crops, (C) forest, (D) range, (E) urban. (Source: NRI) (continued to next page)

(D)

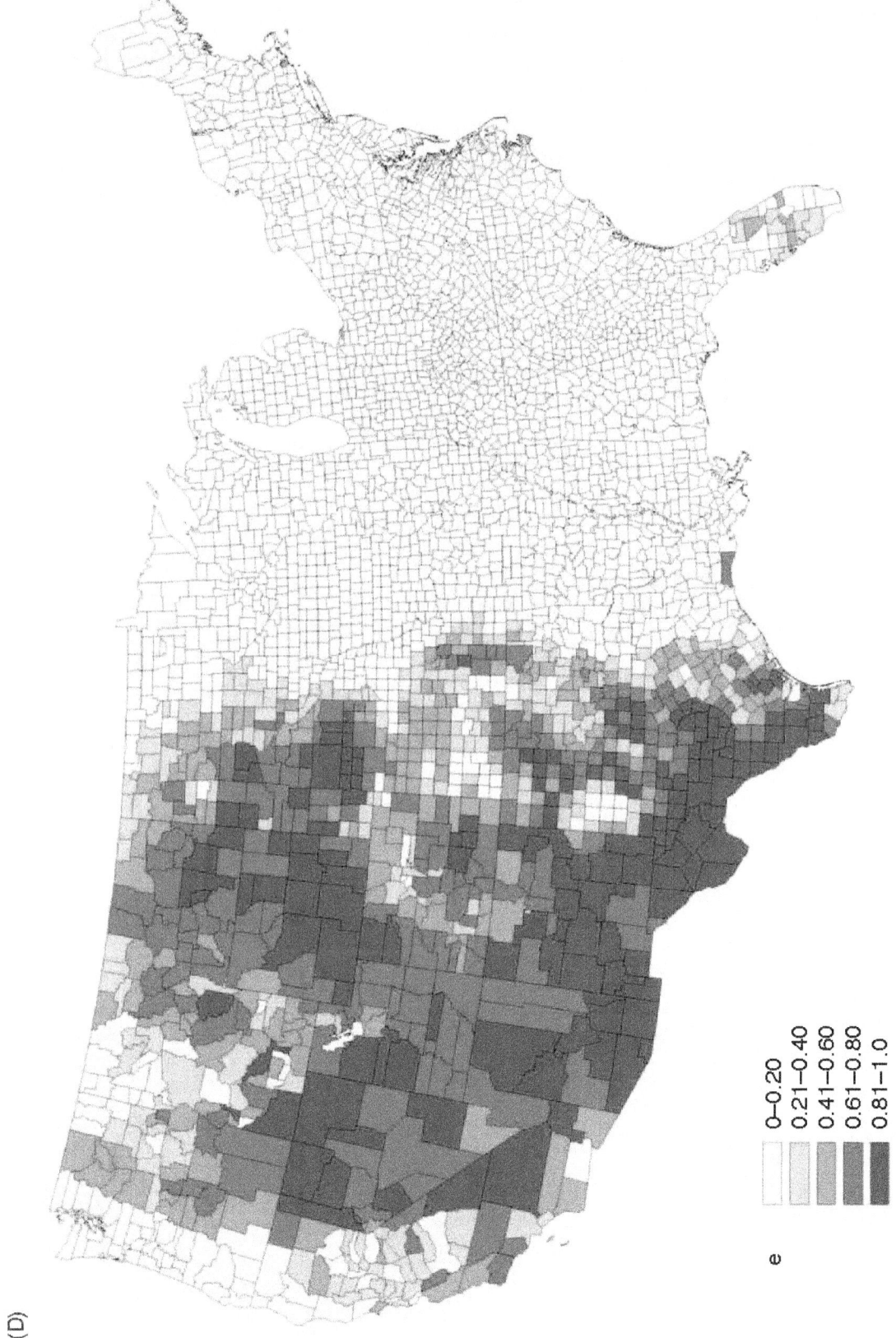

0—0.20
0.21—0.40
0.41—0.60
0.61—0.80
0.81—1.0

e

Figure 2 (continued)—Concentration of five land uses (proportion of each county) on nonfederal land, 1997: (A) pasture, (B) crops, (C) forest, (D) range, (E) urban. (Source: NRI) (continued to next page)

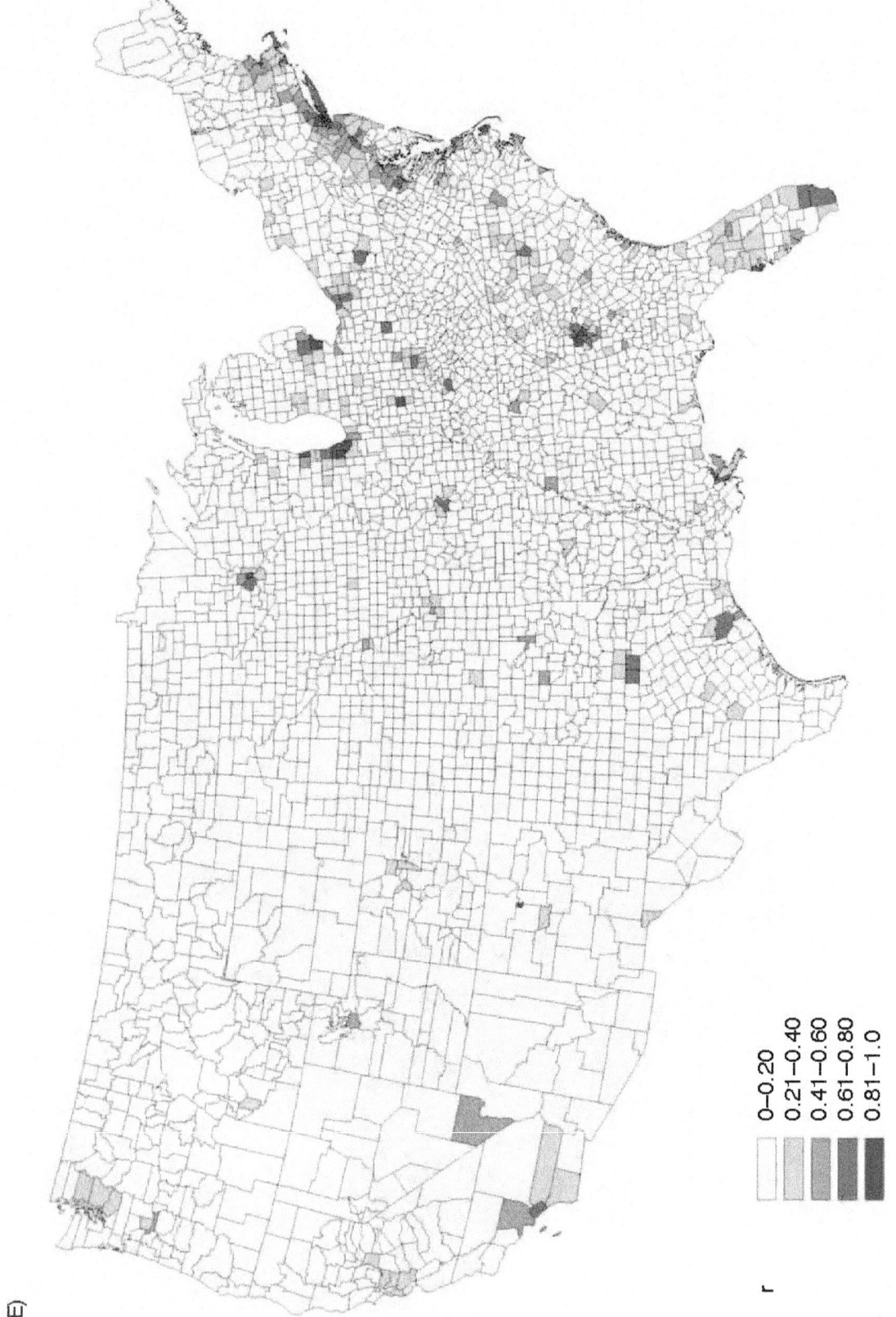

(E)

0—0.20
0.21—0.40
0.41—0.60
0.61—0.80
0.81—1.0

Figure 2 (continued)—Concentration of five land uses (proportion of each county) on nonfederal land, 1997: (A) pasture, (B) crops, (C) forest, (D) range, (E) urban. (Source: NRI)

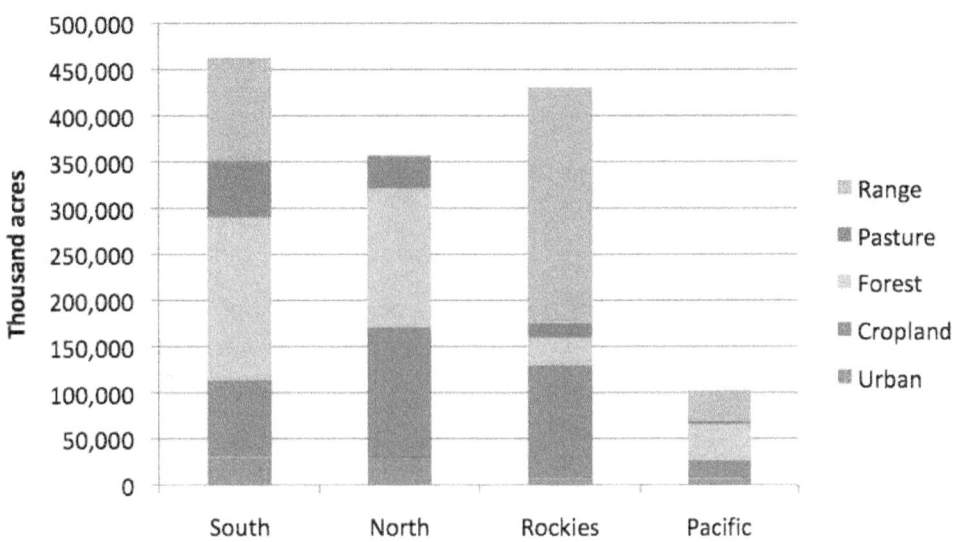

Figure 3—Distribution of land uses within Assessment Regions, 1997. (Source: NRI)

# 2010 RPA ASSESSMENT SCENARIOS

Future renewable resource conditions are influenced by a number of common driving forces such as population change, economic growth, and land use change. Three scenarios in the RPA Assessment are used to characterize the common demographic, socioeconomic and technological driving forces underlying changes in resource conditions and to evaluate the sensitivity of resource trends to a feasible future range of these driving forces. The use of scenarios links the underlying assumptions of the analyses of various resource conditions and uses, and frames the future uncertainty in these driving forces within the integrated modeling and analysis framework of the 2010 RPA Assessment (see text box).

The three RPA scenarios are linked to globally consistent and well-documented scenarios used in the Intergovernmental Panel on Climate Change (IPCC) 4th Assessment (AR4) (IPCC 2007). The scenarios include a range of future global and U.S. socioeconomic and climate conditions likely to affect future U.S. resource conditions and trends (Nakicenovic and others 2000). The IPCC AR4 scenario labels (A1B, A2, and B2) have been maintained in the 2010 RPA Assessment documentation for continuity. The IPCC AR4 global data were scaled to the U.S. national level and sub-national levels for the 2010 RPA Assessment. U.S. gross domestic product (GDP) and population projections used in AR4 analyses were updated, and U.S. population and disposable personal income data were then downscaled to the U.S. county level (Zarnoch and others 2010). While not a part of land use models, the climate output generated from several global circulation models (GCMs) for the scenarios were downscaled to the county scale (Coulson and others 2010) and used in other components of the RPA Assessment.

Population and personal income projections for the three scenarios (A1B, A2, and B2) drive our forecasts of urbanization. The A1B population forecasts are based on 2004 Census projections for the entire United States, while A2 and B2 depart from these forecasts as described below. Zarnoch and others (2010) developed county-scale projections for each scenario based on forecasts from Woods and Poole's (2007) spatial econometric/demographic model which are generally consistent with the A1B projection for 2000-2030. County-level projections between 2030 and 2060 were disaggregated by extending historical patterns of growth from the Woods and Poole projections (see Zarnoch and others 2010 for details). Projections for A2 and B2 applied the same spatial pattern of population change, but were adjusted to yield county-level projections that add up to the national totals for the respective scenarios.

As shown in figures 4 and 5, A1B corresponds to mid range population growth and the highest per capita disposable personal income level of the three IPCC scenarios. Under this scenario, the United States population will be about 446 million with per capita personal income around $80,000 by 2060. Scenario A2 projects the highest population growth, reaching more than 500 million people by 2060, and the lowest projected per capita personal income, around $56,000. Scenario B2 projects the lowest population growth and mid level personal income, predicting a population of 397 million people with per capita personal income around $60,000.

Population is not forecast to grow evenly across the US. Rather, most projected growth occurs around a number of existing urban centers (fig. 6). In addition, a large number of counties are expected to experience population declines (fig. 6 shows these counties in green for Scenario A1B). Population loss is forecasted to be especially high through the Great Plains and Corn Belt, within the Mississippi Alluvial Valley in the South, and in a band from northern Indiana to upstate New York.

# The U.S. Forest Assessment System:
# Modeling for the 2010 RPA Assessment

Land use models represent one component of the U.S. Forest Assessment System (USFAS), a set of computer models designed to forecast alternative futures for the Nation's forests. The USFAS provides a forward looking adjunct to the Nation's Forest Inventory System implemented by the Forest Inventory and Analysis (FIA) Research Program of the U.S. Forest Service. The FIA system is a nationwide monitoring system of repeated inventories that provides for consistent tracking of inventories over time at a high level of detail. The USFAS accounts for changes driven by multiple drivers including biological, physical and human factors. These models address the influence of changing climate, market-driven timber harvesting, and land use changes along with changes driven by the natural succession of forest conditions.

Figure B1 shows a general schematic of this modeling system. The first column describes the input of data beginning with internally consistent combinations of social, economic, and technology forecasts defined as scenarios. The scenarios are linked to various General Circulation Models (climate models) to provide climate forecasts consistent with each scenario. Forest inventory data defines the starting conditions for all forested plots.

The middle column of Figure B1 provides a general picture of the modeling framework. Future forest conditions are driven by biological dynamics—e.g., growth and mortality—which are affected by climate factors. In addition, human choices regarding allocations among land uses, disposal of forest land, timber harvesting, and forest management also affect changes in forests. The interplay of these factors yields the outputs described in the right column where forest projections are consistent with the flow of forest products and land uses. Changes in several other ecosystem services, including water and biodiversity, can also be derived from the forecasted changes in forest conditions and land uses.

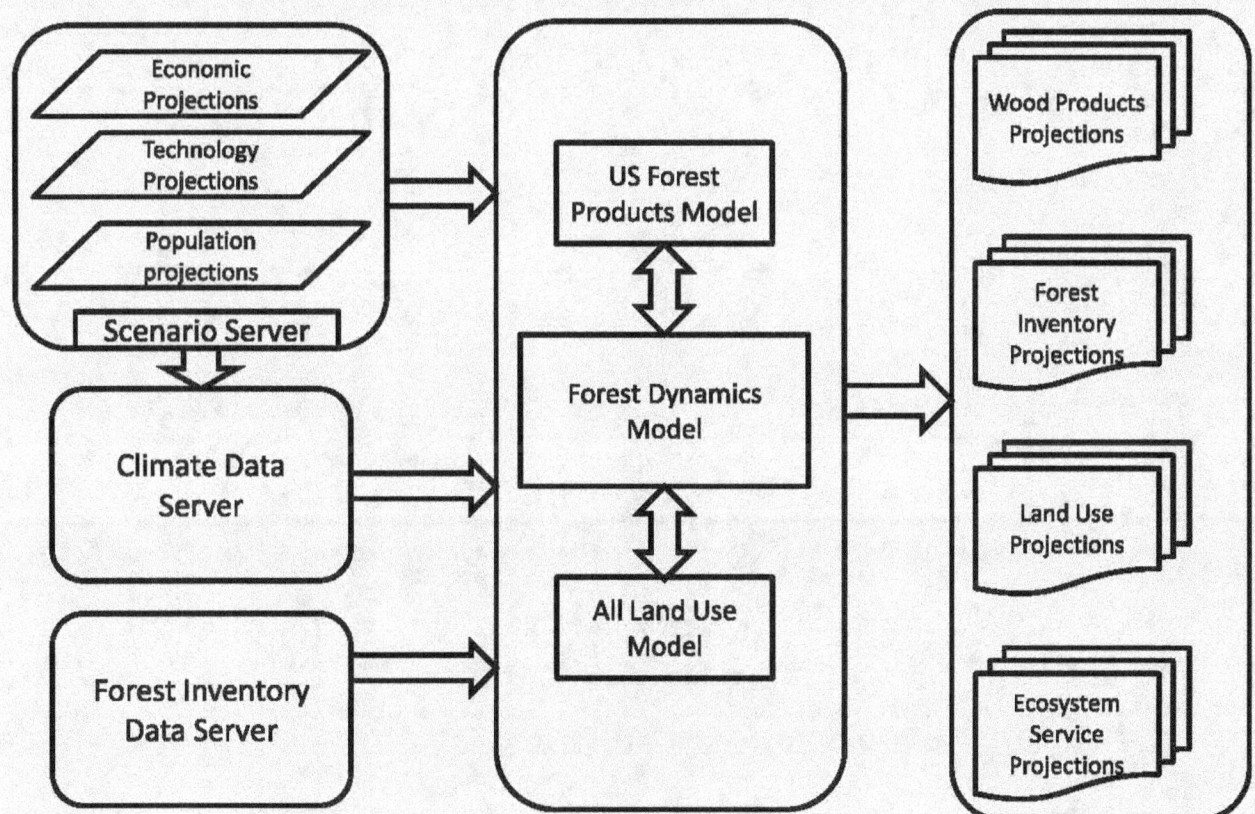

Figure B1 — Schematic of the U.S. Forest Assessment System.

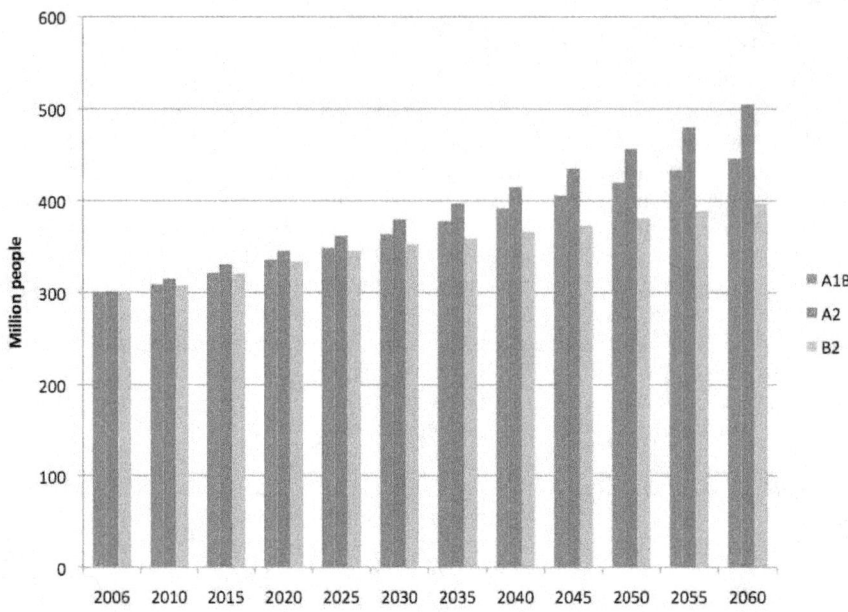

Figure 4—Forecasted U.S. population for three RPA Scenarios (A1B, A2, B2), 2006-2060.

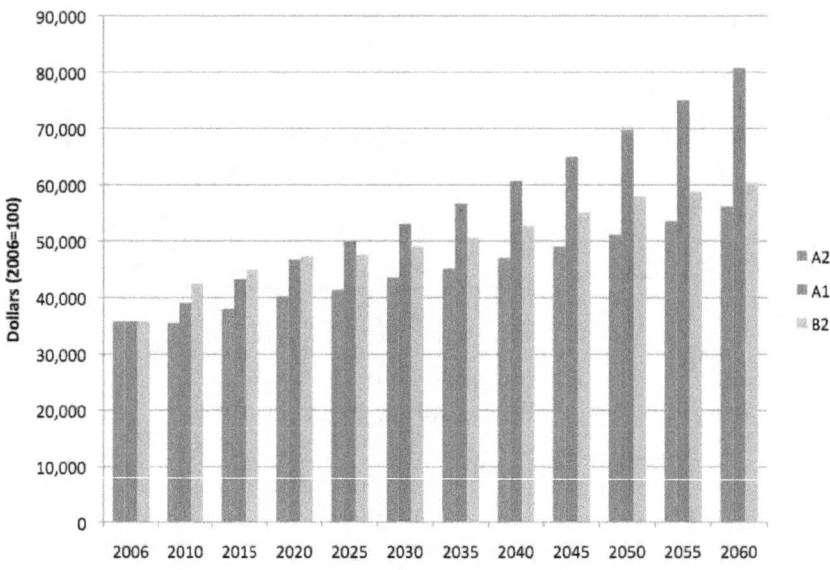

Figure 5—Forecasted per capita personal income for three RPA Scenarios (A1B, A2, B2), 2006-2060.

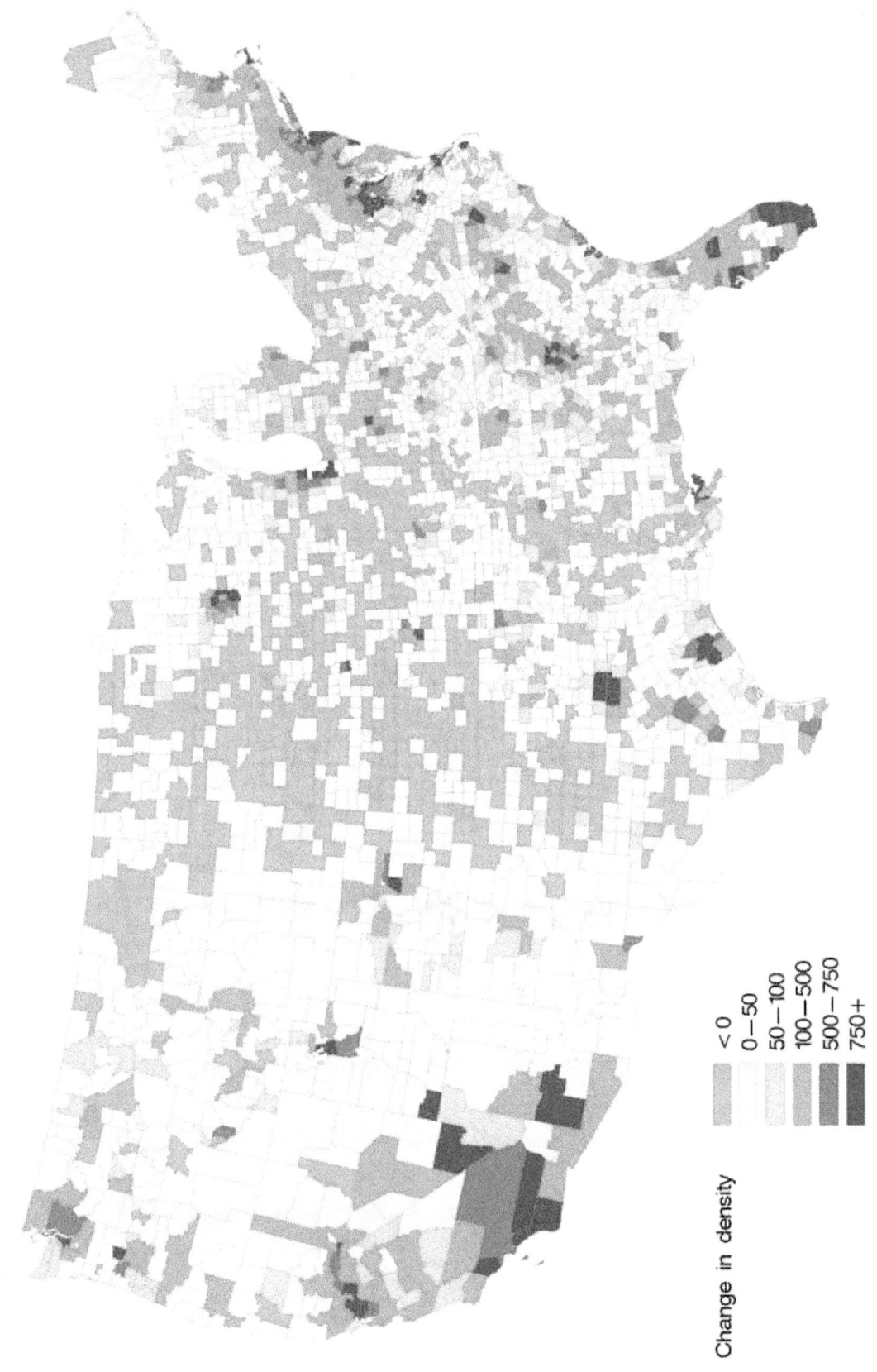

Change in density

<0
0—50
50—100
100—500
500—750
750+

Figure 6—Forecasted change in population density (people per square mile), 1997-2060, for the A1B Scenario. Areas in green are forecasted to experience population declines over this period.

# FORECASTS OF LAND USE CHANGES

We forecasted urban land use changes in response to the population and income futures defined for each of the three scenarios (fig. 7). Scenario A1B, with an intermediate level of population growth but strong growth in personal income, yields the highest rate of urbanization: an increase of 86 million acres by 2060. Scenario B2, with the lowest income and lowest population growth has the lowest rate of urbanization (an increase of 59 million by 2060), and A2, with the highest population growth but intermediate income growth, yields an intermediate rate of urbanization (an increase of 75 million acres by 2060). Urban uses in 1997 totaled 73 million acres, so forecasts show a rough doubling of urban area by 2060 with scenario A2 and increases of 118 percent and 81 percent with scenarios A1B and B2, respectively (see appendix C for detailed forecast results).

The total area of urbanization is similar across the three scenarios until 2040, after which urbanization diverges among the scenarios (fig. 7). In the earlier years when the population differences across scenarios are quite small, urbanization is somewhat faster in scenario B2 because of its higher per capita income. After 2040, rates of urbanization are especially affected by income growth as urban growth for Scenario A1B (where population gains are intermediate but income growth is high) far exceeds the rate for Scenario A2 (where population growth is highest, but income growth is low).

Urban growth varies by region (fig. 8). About 48 percent of urban growth forecasted for A1B is contained in the South (+42 million acres). The North gains about 27 million acres by 2060, while the Rockies and Pacific gain 11 and 8 million acres respectively. Urban area in the Rockies is projected to

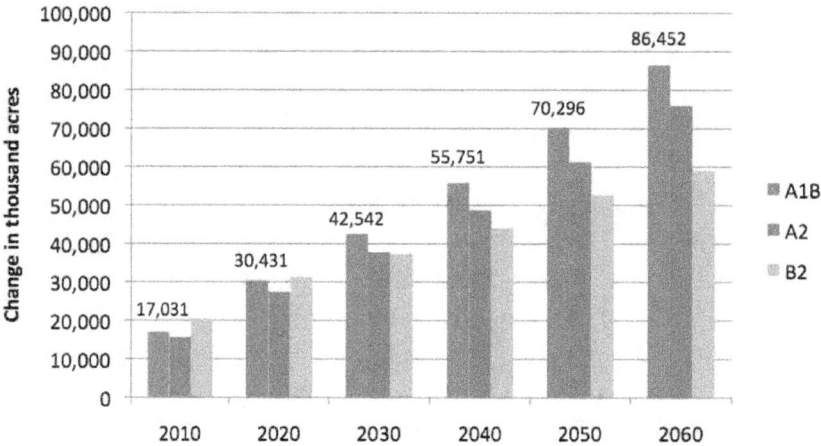

Figure 7—Forecasted change in urban land uses for the United States from a base year of 1997, 2010-2060, by Scenario (numbers are for A1B Scenario).

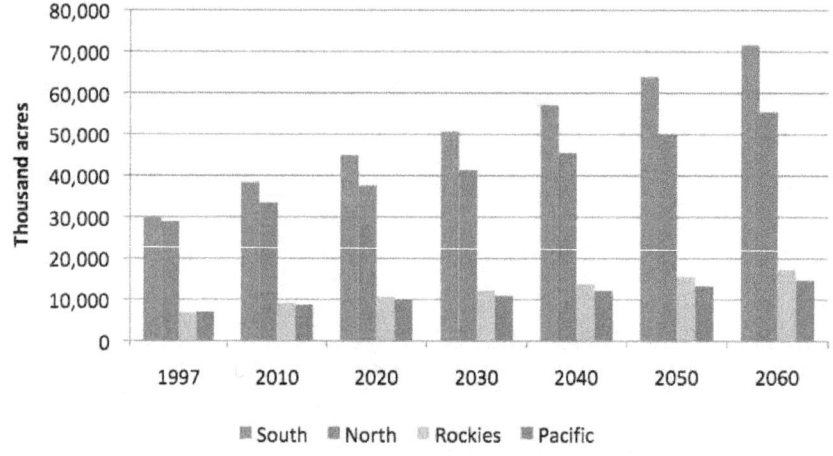

Figure 8—Forecasted urban area by region, 1997-2060, for the A1B scenario.

increase by the highest percentage (+153 percent), followed by the South (+140 percent), the Pacific (+109 percent), and the North (+110 percent). Thus, under A1B, all regions experience at least a doubling of urban area.

Within each region, urbanization is concentrated in some key areas (figs. 9 and 10). For the A1B scenario, the models forecast extensive development in three portions of the North: along the Atlantic seaboard in the northeast, between the lower peninsula of Michigan and the Ohio River, and between Minneapolis, MN and Chicago, IL. Additionally, the models forecast smaller areas of development in southern Missouri and in the New England states of Massachusetts, New Hampshire, and Vermont. Compared to A1B, the B2 scenario shows similar patterns of growth, but shrinks the total area experiencing development (fig. 10). A2 also has a similar pattern of growth with total change intermediate between A1B and B2.

In the South, development is projected to be especially strong in the Southern Appalachian Mountains and the adjacent Piedmont, roughly within a triangle formed by the cities of Raleigh, NC, Atlanta, GA, and Knoxville TN. Texas is forecasted to experience strong growth in a triangular area formed by the cities of Austin, Dallas, and Houston. Much of Florida is forecast to experience extensive development, especially along the Gulf and Atlantic coasts. Nashville, the Gulf Coast, northern Kentucky, and northern Virginia are also forecasted to grow strongly over this period.

While growth is spread across fairly broad areas of the East, it is much more isolated in the West. The growth forecasted for the Rocky Mountain region is focused in four areas: Denver and the Front Range of Colorado, Albuquerque, NM, Las Vegas, NV and St. George, UT, and Salt Lake City, UT. In the Pacific Region, urban growth is focused within the Seattle-Portland region, the San Francisco Bay area, and southern California.

Increases in urban land are reflected in declines for all other land uses (fig. 11). For A1B, forests are forecasted to decline by about 37 million acres (10 percent), cropland by 28 million acres (8 percent), and pasture by 9 million (8 percent) and rangeland by 12 million acres (3 percent) respectively. We explore the forecasts for each of these rural land uses across the three scenarios next.

## Forest Land Uses

Change in forest area varies substantially across the scenarios: A1B forecasts a loss of 38 million acres by 2060, A2 forecasts a loss of 32 million acres, and B2 forecasts a loss of 25 million acres. In terms of both area and percent, the South is forecasted to experience the greatest decline in forest area by 2060 (figs. 12 and 13). For the A1B Scenario, southern forests would decline by about 21 million acres (12 percent) between 1997 and 2060, while the North would lose about 12 million acres (8 percent), and the Rockies and Pacific would lose 1 million acres (4 percent) and 3 million acres (8 percent) respectively. Because the majority of forest land in the West is public, and therefore held fixed, the forecasted change in total (public and nonpublic) forest area for the western regions is < 1 percent.

Forecasted forest losses are concentrated in a few subregions of the United States (figs. 14 and 15). Within the South Region, forest losses are especially concentrated in the Southern Appalachian Mountains and the Piedmont—Northern Georgia, central North Carolina, and eastern Tennessee show especially high rates of forest loss. Elsewhere in the South, forest losses are concentrated along the coasts. In the North, forest losses are concentrated in a large area centered on Philadelphia and extending into New Jersey, Maryland, Delaware, and southern New York. Other smaller concentrations of forest loss in the North include an area stretching from Boston north into Vermont and the northern half of Michigan's Lower Peninsula. In the Pacific Region, forest losses are concentrated in areas between Portland, OR and Seattle, WA and between San Francisco, CA and Reno, NV. In the Rockies, areas of forest losses are focused around Salt Lake City, UT and the Front Range of Colorado.

## Cropland Uses

Forecasts of cropland loss range from 19 million acres for the B2 Scenario to about 28 million acres for the A1B Scenario (fig. 16). About 85 percent of cropland losses (24 million acres) are contained in the eastern assessment regions, with nearly an equal split between the South and the North. The largest region of cropland loss extends from southern Michigan southwest to the Lower Mississippi

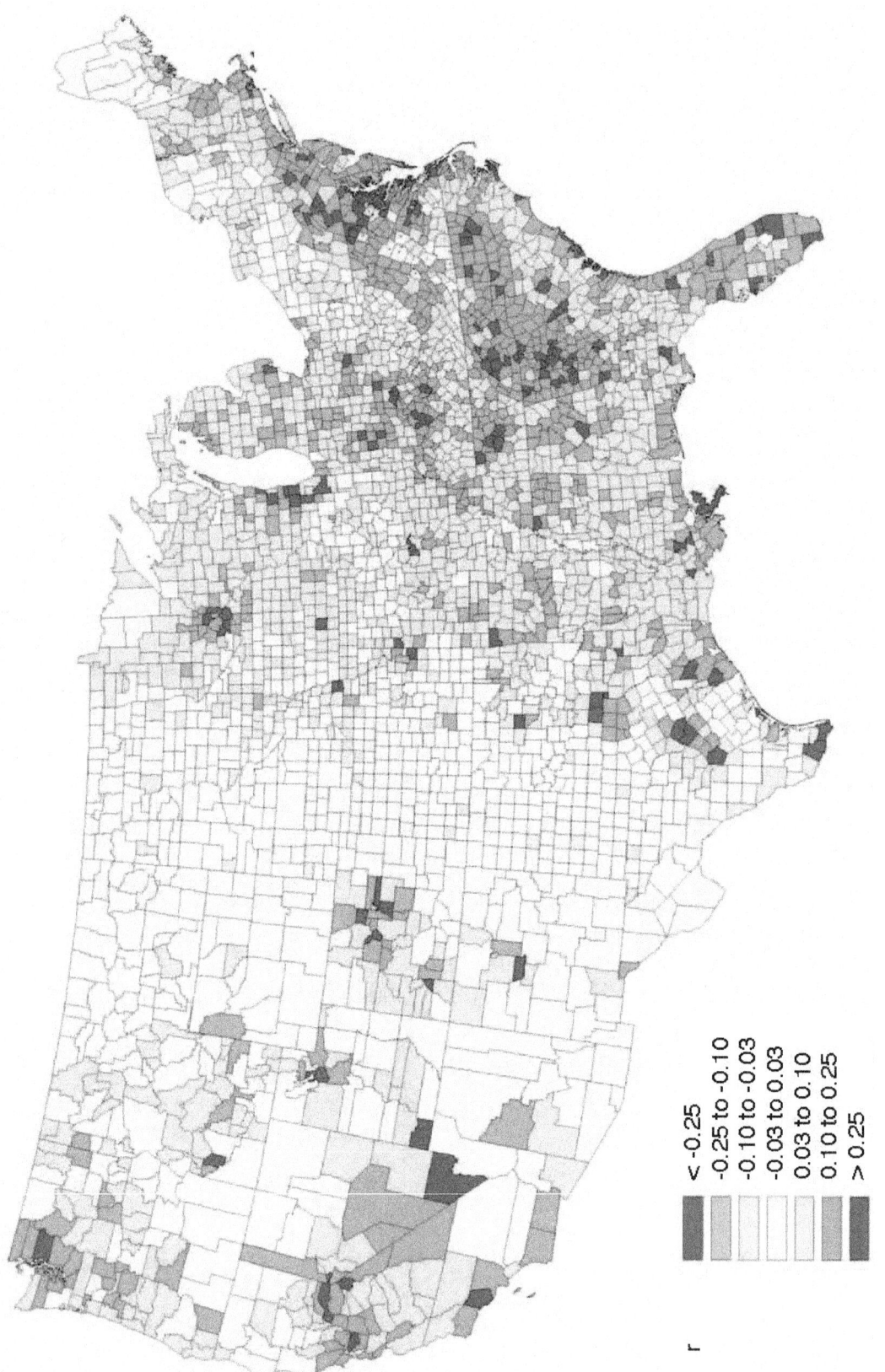

-0.25
-0.25 to -0.10
-0.10 to -0.03
-0.03 to 0.03
0.03 to 0.10
0.10 to 0.25
> 0.25

Figure 9—Forecasted change in proportion of county in the urban land use, A1B Scenario, 1997-2060.

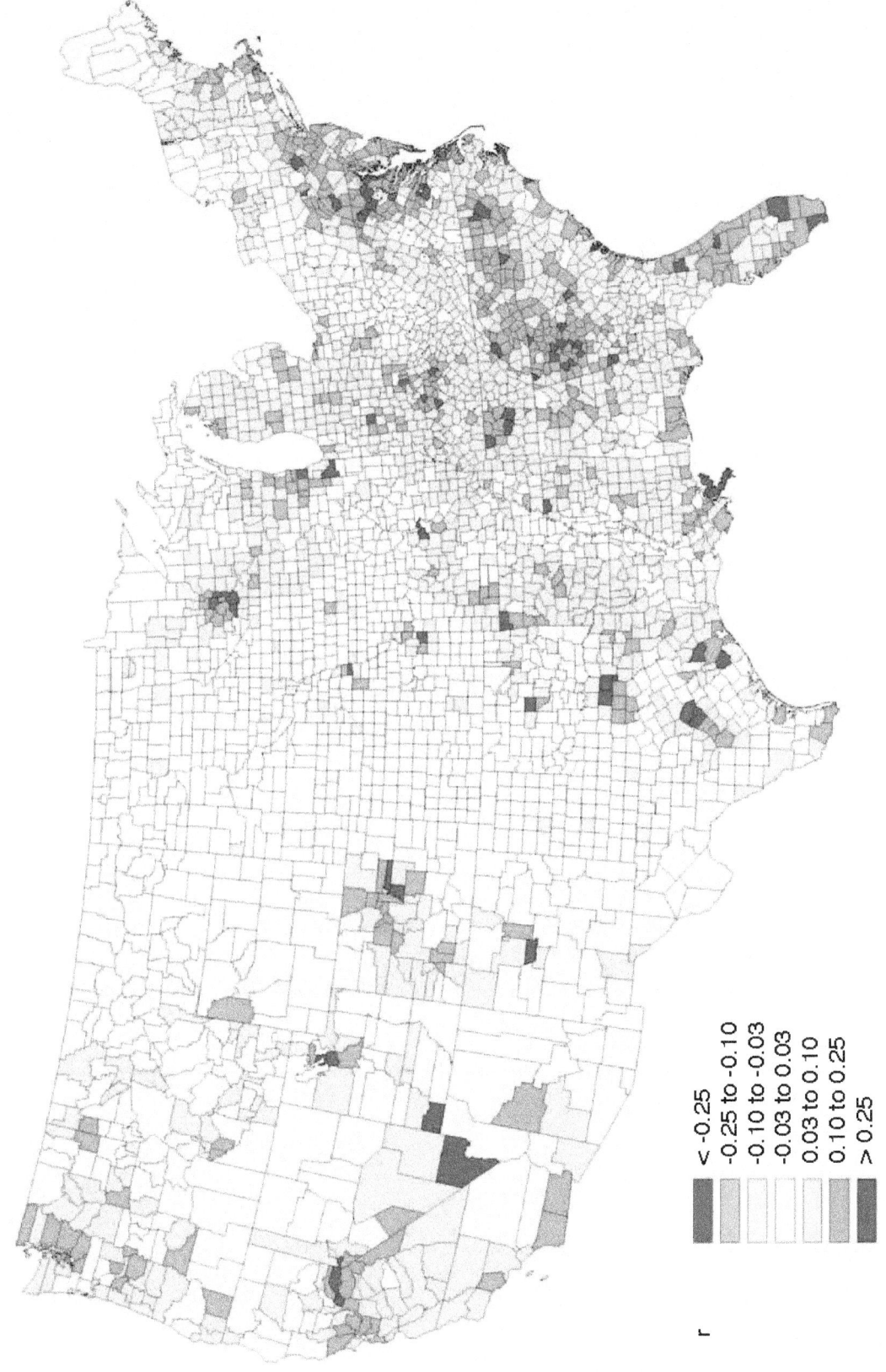

Figure 10—Forecasted change in the proportion of county in urban land use, B2 Scenario, 1997-2060.

| | |
|---|---|
| | < -0.25 |
| | -0.25 to -0.10 |
| | -0.10 to -0.03 |
| | -0.03 to 0.03 |
| | 0.03 to 0.10 |
| | 0.10 to 0.25 |
| | > 0.25 |

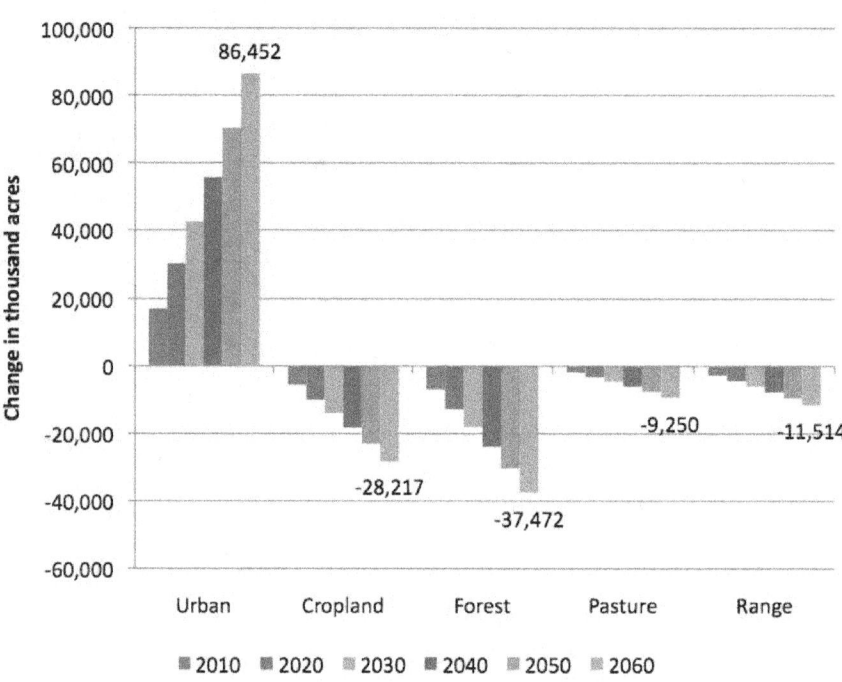

Figure 11—Forecasted change in the areas of major nonfederal land uses, A1B Scenario, 2010-2060, compared to 1997.

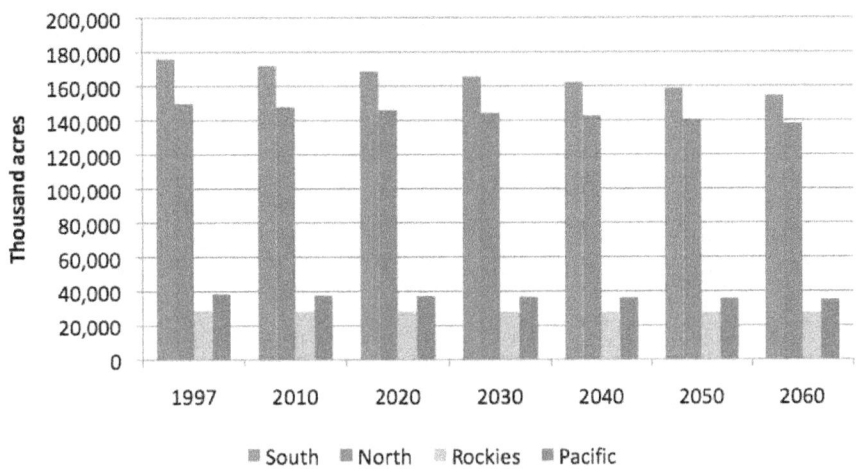

Figure 12—Forecasted forest area by region, 1997-2060, A1B Scenario.

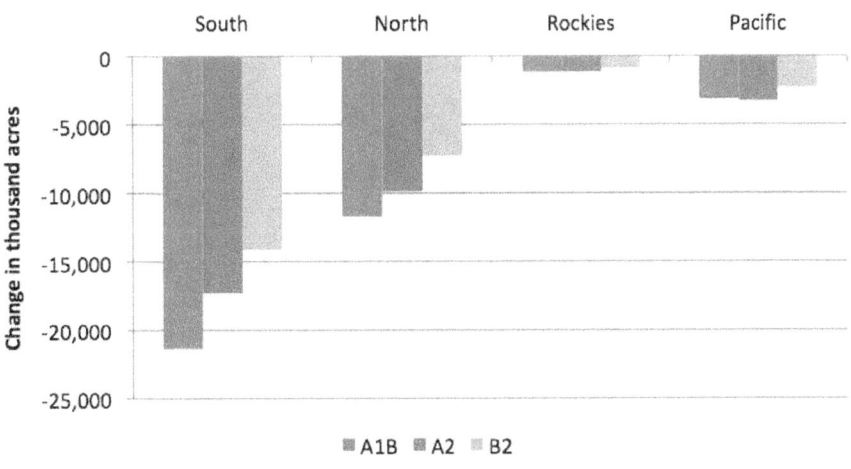

Figure 13—Forecasted change in nonfederal forest area, 1997-2060, by RPA Scenario (A1B, A2, B2).

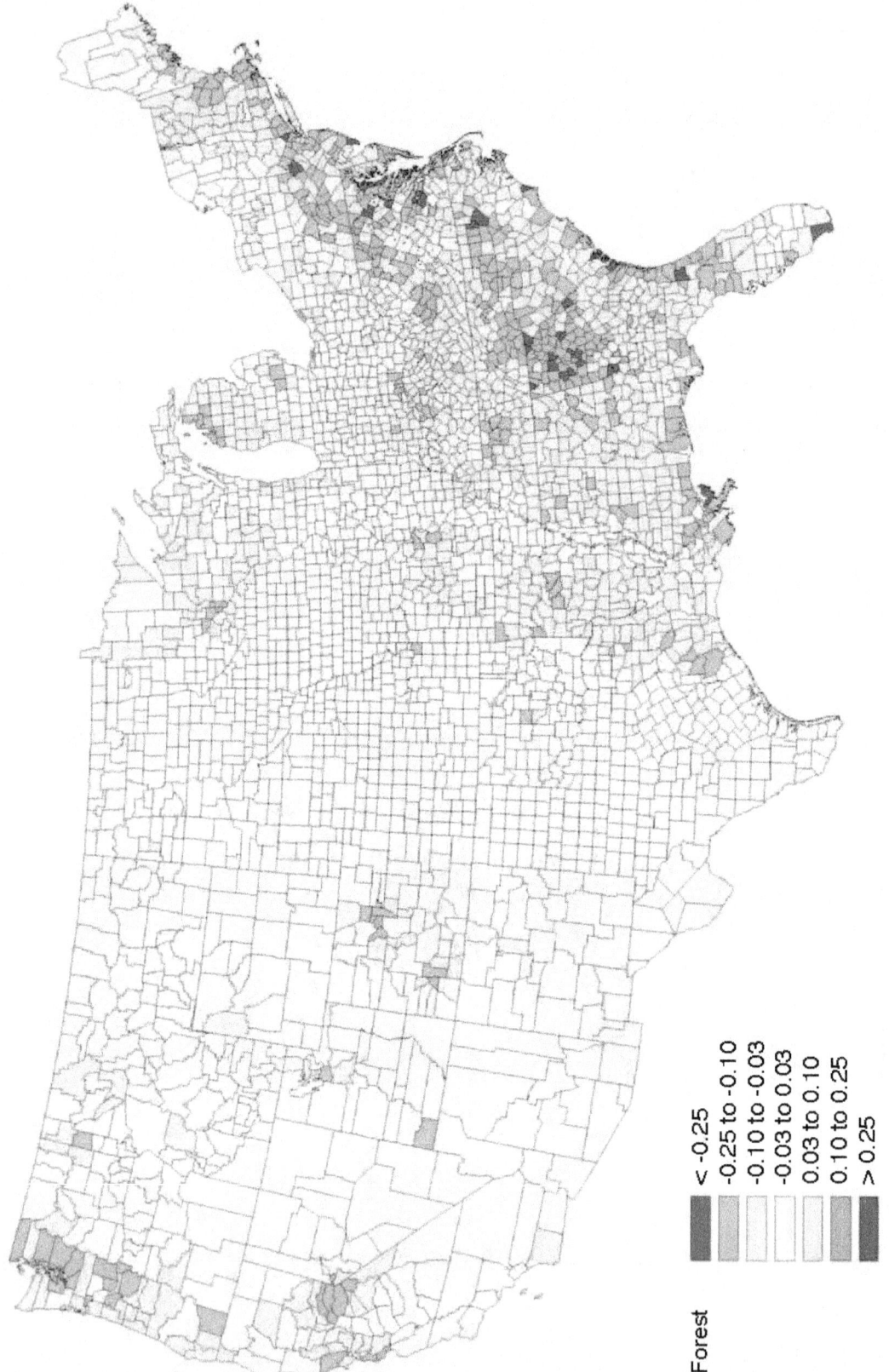

Forest

| | |
|---|---|
| | < -0.25 |
| | -0.25 to -0.10 |
| | -0.10 to -0.03 |
| | -0.03 to 0.03 |
| | 0.03 to 0.10 |
| | 0.10 to 0.25 |
| | > 0.25 |

Figure 14—Forecasted change in proportion of county that is in forest use, A1B Scenario, 1997-2060.

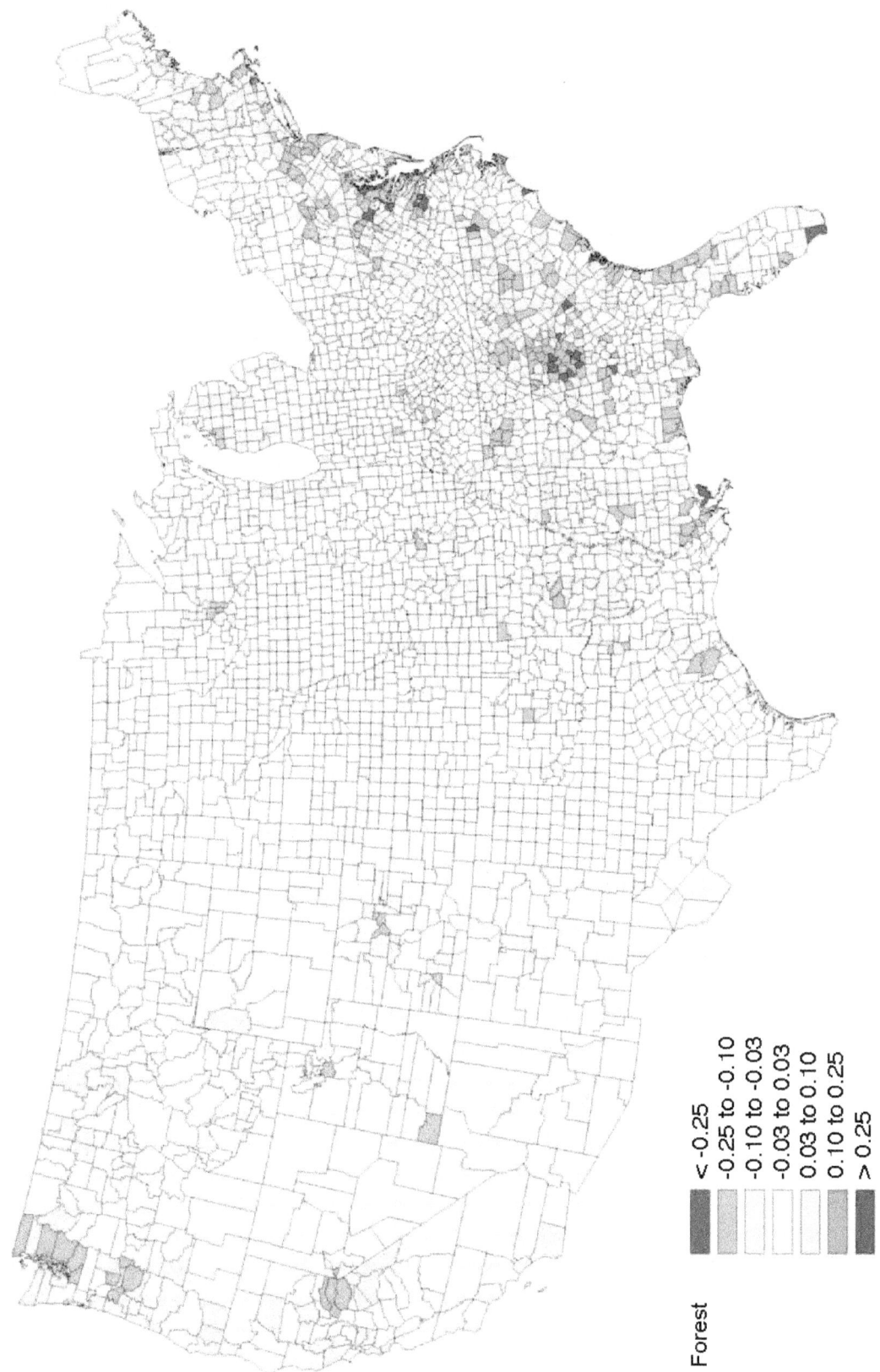

Forest

- < -0.25
- -0.25 to -0.10
- -0.10 to -0.03
- -0.03 to 0.03
- 0.03 to 0.10
- 0.10 to 0.25
- > 0.25

Figure 15—Forecasted change in proportion of county that is in forest use, 1997-2060, B2 Scenario.

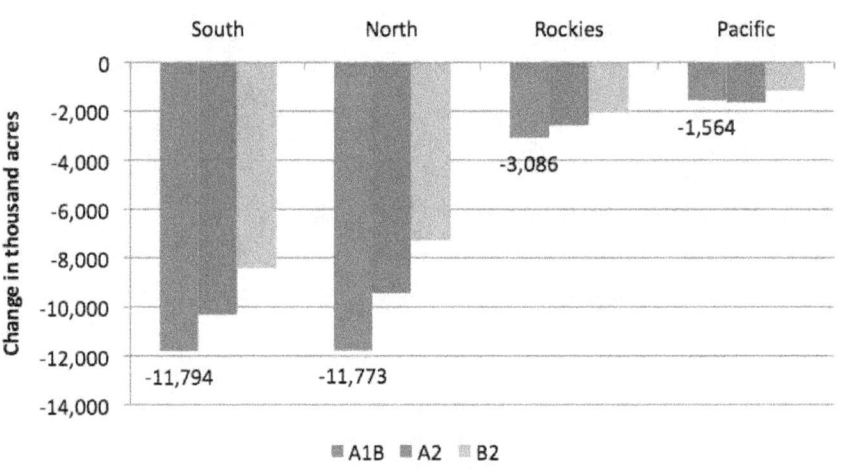

Figure 16—Forecasted change in the area of cropland by RPA Scenario (A1B, A2, B2), 1997-2060.

Alluvial Valley and includes much of western Kentucky, Indiana, and Ohio (figs. 17 and 18). Other focal areas for cropland loss are eastern North Carolina, the eastern seaboard between New York City, NY and Washington, DC, areas surrounding Chicago, IL and Minneapolis, MN the coastline between Houston, TX and New Orleans, LA, and southern Florida. In the West, cropland losses are much more limited and isolated with some notable declines in southern California, central Washington, and around Salt Lake City, UT.

## Rangeland Uses

Forecasts of rangeland losses extend from 8 million acres under the B2 Scenario to 12 million acres for the A1B Scenario (fig. 19). Roughly one half of rangeland losses occur in the Rockies region with the remainder in the South and Pacific regions. In the Rockies, rangeland losses are forecasted for Colorado and parts of Utah and Arizona (figs. 20 and 21). In the South, nearly all of the rangeland losses are found in Texas, while most of the losses in the Pacific are in southern California. The very small area of rangeland found in the North is held fixed within the modeling framework (see appendix A).

## Rural Land Use Flexibility

Our three scenarios provide alternative realizations of the future based on different projections of population and economic growth. Future landscape patterns could also be shaped by a number of other factors, including bioenergy policies and technological developments that would favor either wood or other feedstocks in the production of liquid biofuels or the burning of wood for the generation of electricity. Climate policies that allow trading of the carbon sequestered on forest lands could also affect landowners' land use and management decisions. These policy futures, and their interactions with changes in markets for wood products and crops could produce structural changes in rural land markets.

While marginal demand changes can be effectively modeled using econometric specifications such as the one developed here, structural changes could exceed the information content of these models. Rather than attempt to model the impacts of these types of structural changes—i.e., changes in rural land rents that far exceed historical precedent— we use an index of land use complexity to indicate where future land use changes might be especially sensitive to changes in these markets. We posit that the potential for broad scale land use changes would likely be concentrated in areas where current land use is highly diverse. Since the marginal returns to alternative uses in areas with diverse land use patterns are likely to be similar (thereby explaining the diversity of land use choices within the area), small differences in land rents could result in land use switching. We construct a measure of land use diversity to map the distribution of these complex landscapes.

Our measure of diversity or flexibility starts with the premise that land use switching is most likely in places where current land uses vary within a county. The potential for switching between crop uses and forests is likely to be greatest where both crop and forest uses currently coexist. This correspondence between diversity and substitutability could reflect both biophysical factors such as soil productivity and demand factors such as access to markets. In either case, the probability of land use conversions may correlate with a measure of this complexity.

Our rural land use complexity index has two important elements: the proportion of land within a county that is rural and the diversity of rural land uses (see appendix B for details). The index incorporates three land use aggregates: (1) undeveloped rural uses, equal to the sum of forest and range uses, (2) cropland, and (3) pastureland. The index ranges between 0 and 1 and reaches its maximum when the entire county is rural and there is an equal split between the three use classes—cropland, pasture, and native. Minimum values occur where counties have no rural land or where only one land use dominates the rural area.

A map of the rural land use complexity index (fig. 22) shows that complexity is unevenly distributed and that a few large areas of high complexity are found across the United States. The area with the greatest concentration of complexity includes most of Missouri, western Kentucky, central and western Tennessee and northern Mississippi. Another especially complex rural landscape is contained between prairie and northern mixed forest (Laurentian) ecological provinces in Minnesota and Wisconsin. The Great Plains are generally moderately diverse but rural lands are highly complex in the Cross-Timbers zone in east-central Oklahoma and Texas. Much of southern Idaho and parts of eastern Washington also have high complexity values. In the North smaller areas of high complexity are observed in upstate New York and southeastern Ohio. In the South, a high degree of complexity occurs in south central Florida, southwestern Georgia to southeastern Alabama, and southern Louisiana. These highly complex landscapes provide one measure of where policy shifts could have immediate effects on land use switching.

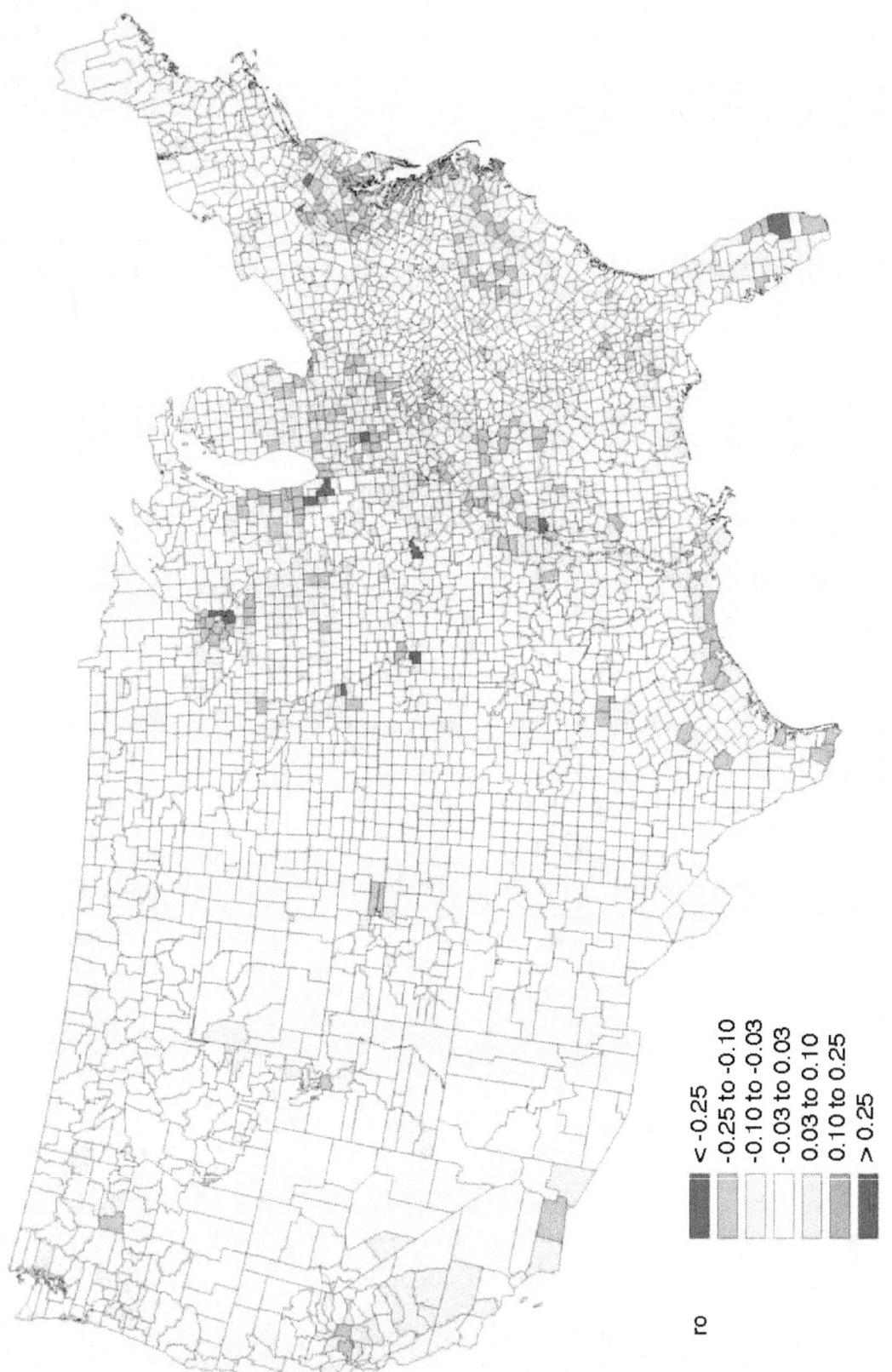

Figure 17—Forecasted change in proportion of county that is in cropland use, A1B Scenario, 1997-2060.

| < -0.25 |
| -0.25 to -0.10 |
| -0.10 to -0.03 |
| -0.03 to 0.03 |
| 0.03 to 0.10 |
| 0.10 to 0.25 |
| > 0.25 |

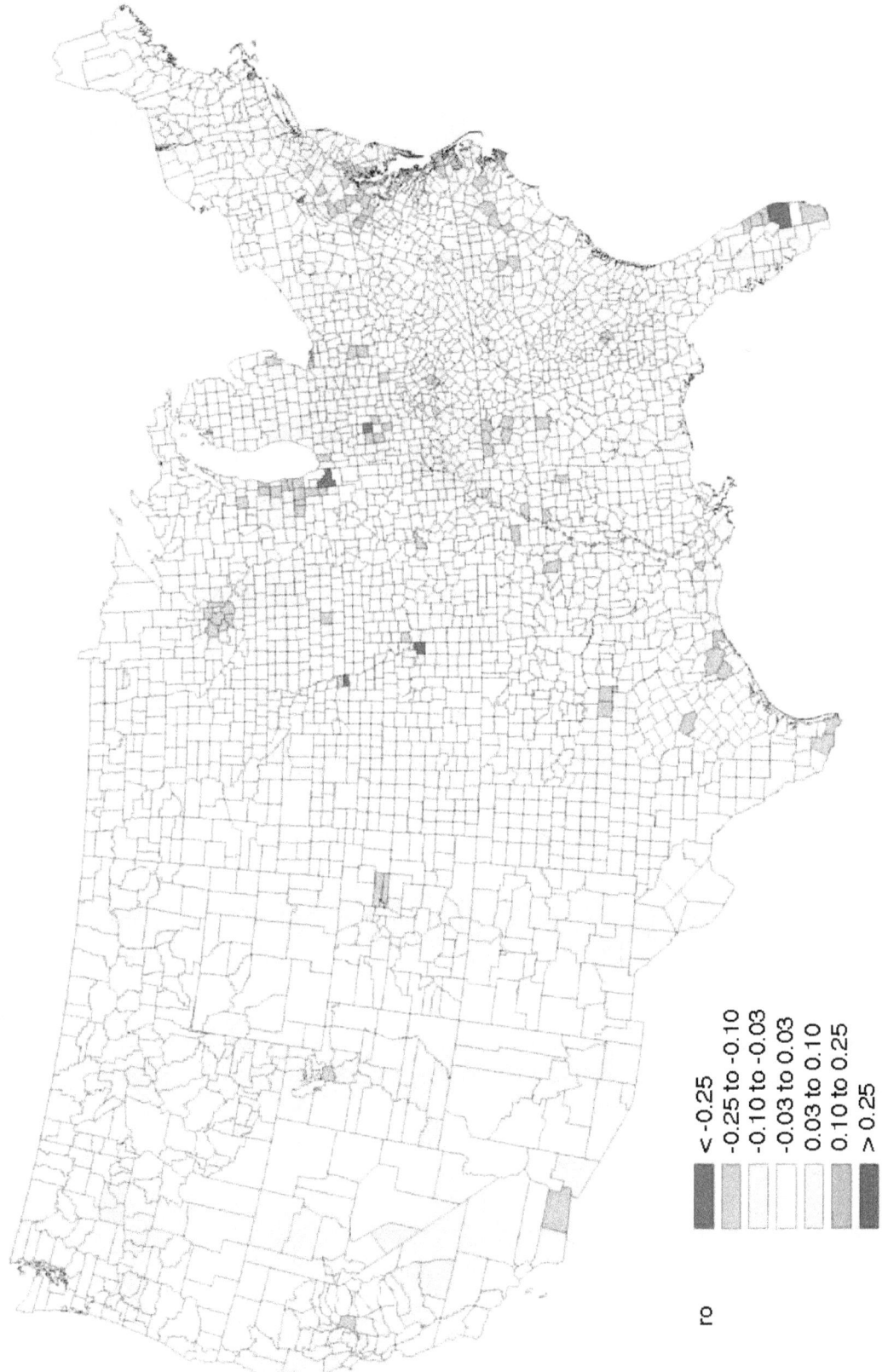

- < -0.25
- -0.25 to -0.10
- -0.10 to -0.03
- -0.03 to 0.03
- 0.03 to 0.10
- 0.10 to 0.25
- > 0.25

Figure 18—Forecasted change in proportion of county that is in cropland use, B2 Scenario, 1997-2060.

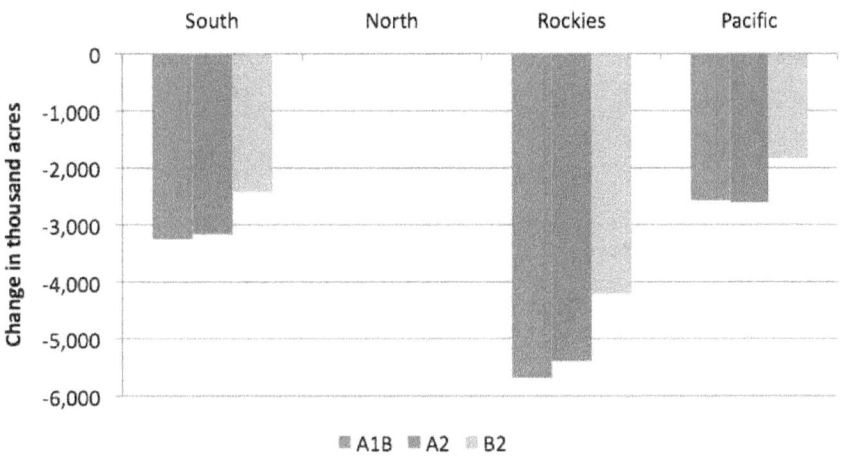

Figure 19—Forecasted change in the area of rangeland by RPA Scenario (A1B, A2, B2), 1997-2060.

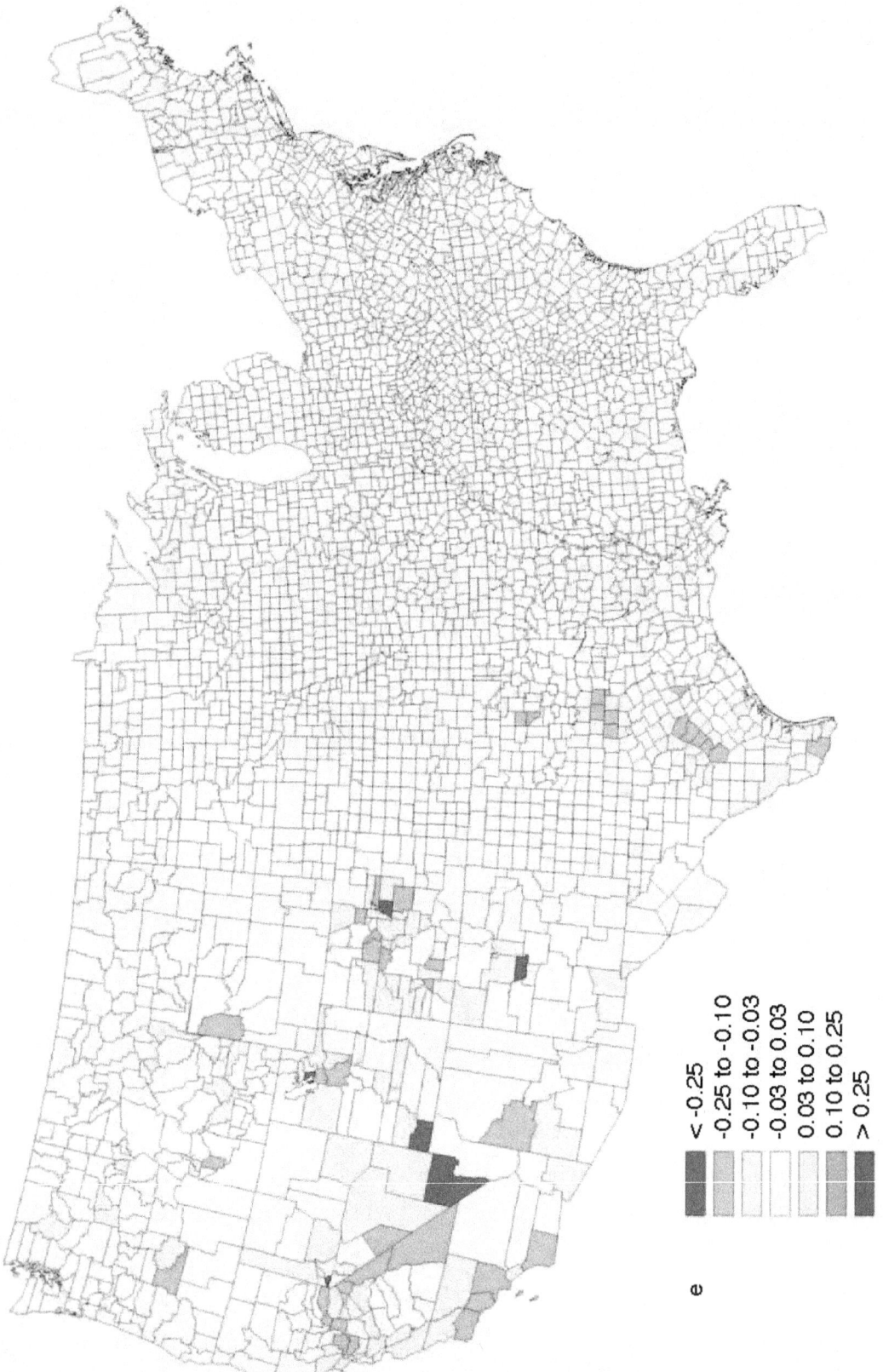

Figure 20—Forecasted change in proportion of county that is in cropland use, 1997-2060, A1B Scenario.

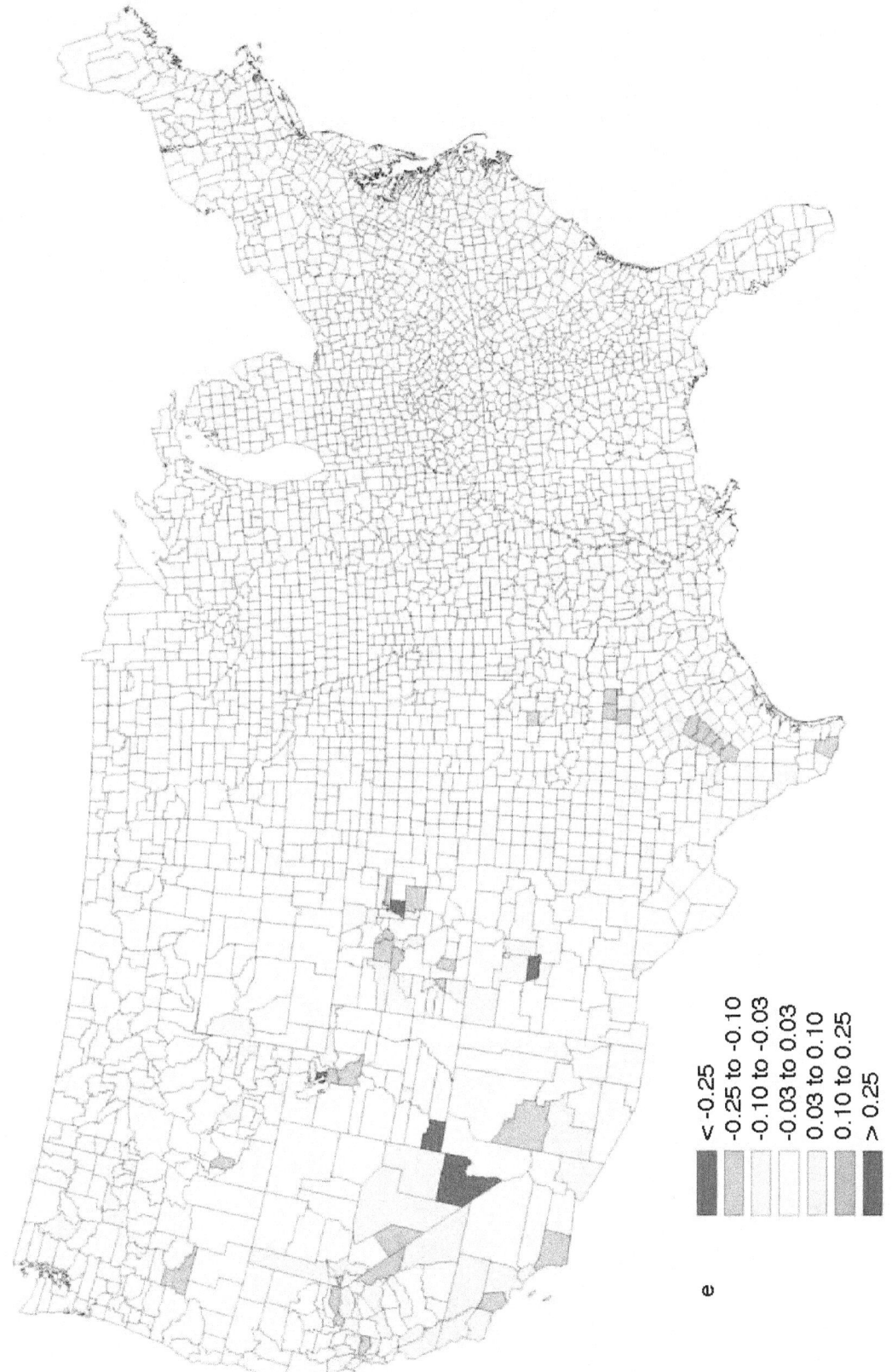

**Legend:**

- < -0.25
- -0.25 to -0.10
- -0.10 to -0.03
- -0.03 to 0.03
- 0.03 to 0.10
- 0.10 to 0.25
- > 0.25

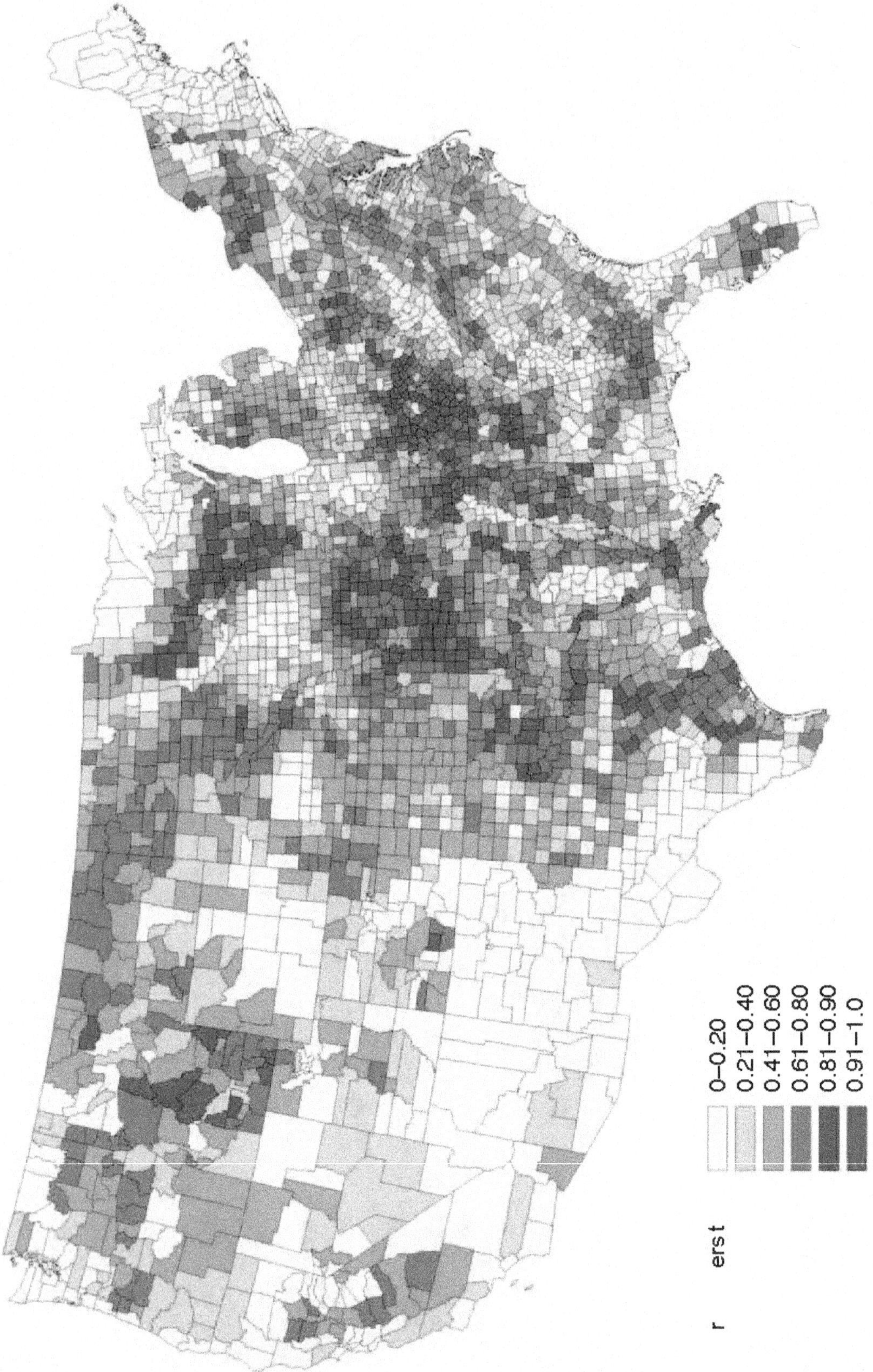

0–0.20
0.21–0.40
0.41–0.60
0.61–0.80
0.81–0.90
0.91–1.0

r    erst

Figure 22—Rural land use complexity index for nonfederal lands, 1997.

## KEY FINDINGS

- **Urbanization**. Between 60 and 86 million acres of rural land are forecasted to be developed between 1997 and 2060, at a rate of 1 to 1.4 million acres per year. With this development comes loss of rural land uses and forests are the greatest source of newly developed land over this period.

- **Forest losses**. Between 24 and 38 million acres of forests are forecasted to be converted to other uses between 1997 and 2060. More than half of the forecasted forest losses occur in the South and more than 90 percent occur in the Eastern United States.

- **Cropland losses**. Cropland losses are forecasted to range between 19 and 28 million acres and would be focused primarily in the Midwest and Mid Atlantic States.

- **Rangeland losses**. Rangeland losses are forecast to range between 8 and 11 million acres and would be focused in Colorado, Nevada, southern California, and central Texas.

- **Rural land use flexibility**. Rural land use complexity is highest in a few areas including Missouri, central Kentucky, the cross-timber region of Oklahoma and Texas, a zone in central Minnesota and Wisconsin, and southern Idaho. Land uses in these areas may be especially variable in response to new policies and structural changes in markets that influence returns to rural land uses.

## LITERATURE CITED

Coulson, D.P.; Joyce, L.A.; Price, D.T. 2010. Climate scenarios for the conterminous United States at the county spatial scale using SRES scenarios A1B and A2 and PRISM climatology. Fort Collins, CO: U.S. Department of Agriculture Forest Service, Rocky Mountain Research Station. http://www.fs.fed.us/rm/data_archive/dataaccess/US_ClimateScenarios_county_A1B_A2_PRISM.shtml. [Date accessed: March 25, 2011].

Intergovernmental Panel on Climate Change [IPCC]. 2007. Climate change 2007, Synthesis Report. 107 p. http://www.ipcc.ch/publications_and_data/publications_ipcc_fourth_assessment_report_synthesis_report.htm. [Date accessed: March 25, 2011].

Nakicenovic, N.; Alcamo, J.; Davis, G. [and others]. 2000. Special report on emissions scenarios: A special report of working group III of the Intergovernmental Panel on Climate Change. Cambridge, UK: Cambridge University Press. 599 p. http://www.grida.no/climate/ipcc/emission/index.htm. [Date accessed: March 25, 2011].

Rudis, V.A. 1999. Ecological subregion codes by county, conterminous United States. Gen. Tech. Rep. SRS–36. Asheville, NC: U.S. Department of Agriculture, Forest Service, Southern Research Station. 95 p.

U.S. Department of Agriculture Forest Service. 2001. 2000 RPA assessment of forest and rangelands. FS-687. Washington, DC: U.S. Department of Agriculture, Forest Service. 78 p.

Wear, D.N. 2010. Forecasting land uses for alternative futures. Draft manuscript. On file with: David Wear at U.S. Department of Agriculture Forest Service, Research Triangle Park Forestry Sciences Laboratory, 3041 Cornwallis Road, Research Triangle Park, NC 27713. 57 p.

Woods and Poole Economics. 2007. Complete Economic Data Source (CEDDS) Technical documentation. Washington, DC: Woods and Poole Economics Inc. 101 p.

Wooldridge, J.M. 2002. Econometric analysis of cross section and panel data. Cambridge, MA: MIT Press. 752 p.

Zarnoch, S.J.; Cordell, H.K.; Betz, C.J.; Langner, L. 2010. Projecting county-level populations under three future scenarios: a technical document supporting the Forest Service 2010 RPA Assessment. e-Gen. Tech. Rep. SRS–128. Asheville, NC: U.S. Department of Agriculture Forest Service, Southern Research Station. 8 p.

# Appendix A—Land Use Change Models

This appendix provides documentation of the land use models used to generate forecasts for this report. Wear (2010) provides details on the modeling approach.

For each county in the coterminous United States, we model the urbanization process and changes in four rural uses: forest, crops, range, and pasture. The dataset used for model estimations is a panel of observed land uses in 2 years (1987 and 1997), the most recent comprehensive dataset available from the NRI land use inventory. Models were applied to what we define as the variable or mutable land base: nonfederal land classified as developed, crops, pasture, range, or forests. All other land in the county was held fixed in its current use. A two-stage modeling approach first defines urban-rural allocations and then allocates land among the four rural land uses.

We assume that the demand for urban uses dominates all other land uses. That is, we expect that the amount of urban land use is determined by demand factors that influence urban land rents and is unaffected by competition with any other land use. Consider the following reduced form model:

$$U = \left( \overline{\phantom{-}} \ \overline{\phantom{-}} \ \overline{\phantom{-}} \right) \qquad (1)$$

where:
$U$ = the area in urban use
$\overline{\phantom{-}}$ = a vector of time-varying variables from the RPA scenarios, including the population contained in the county (pop), and the real per capita disposable income for the county (inc). These variables change within each RPA scenario
$\overline{\phantom{-}}$ and $\overline{\phantom{-}}$ = vectors of observed and unobserved time-invariant variables respectively, and describe the land quality attributes of the county—for example soil productivity, access to markets, etc.

A linear specification of equation 1 is:

$$U_{it} = \beta + \beta_1 pop_{it} + \beta_2 pop_{it}^2 +$$
$$\beta_3 inc_{it} + \delta \overline{Z}_i + \alpha \overline{X}_i + \varepsilon_{it} \qquad (2)$$

Population and income are expected to be positively associated with the area of urban uses—in effect they proxy for an urban land use rent. To model changes in the area of urban land use, we difference equation 2:

$$U_{it} = U_{t-1} + \beta_1 (pop_{it} - pop_{it-1}) +$$
$$(+)$$
$$\beta_2 (pop_{it}^2 - pop_{it-1}^2) + \beta_3 (inc_{it} - inc_{it-1}) + \varepsilon_{it}^*$$
$$(-) \qquad\qquad (+) \qquad (3)$$

Differencing causes observed and unobserved fixed attributes of the county to fall out of the change equation (see Wooldridge 2002). Change therefore relies strictly on time-varying variables that are forecast to change between periods. Other time-varying variables such as rents accruing to crop or timber uses are excluded from this model by assumption—i.e., that urban rents completely dominate all rural rents in the area of the county affected by the shift in demand. We posit that this urban growth difference equation may differ across subregions of the United States, due in part to the effects of topography and climate on the spatial agglomeration of uses (e.g., mountainous areas and flat areas may reveal different development patterns determined in part by topographic features). We therefore estimated separate models for broad regions and within each regional model we allowed for differences in coefficients by ecological provinces (Rudis 1999) by interacting dummy variables for the ecological provinces with each independent variable.

To address changes in rural land uses we considered three different models with a progression of complexity. The first model simply allocates development among rural uses based on proportion of occurrence—Rent Neutral Urbanization Model. The second model allows the allocation of newly developed land to be skewed from the observed proportions and influenced by the rents accruing to the rural uses based on historical evidence—Rent-Biased Urbanization Model. The third model allows additionally for substitution between rural uses in response to changes in rents—Rural Substitution Model.

## Rent Neutral Urbanization Model

This model assumes that changes in rural land uses are driven exclusively by urbanization and that the probability of a rural use being converted to a developed use is defined by the observed proportion of that land use within the county. Because urban rents dominate rents for rural land uses, developers are indifferent to opportunity or conversion costs of agricultural and forest land uses. In equation form, the changes in cropland ($C$), forest ($F$) and pasture ($P$) uses indexed by time period ($t$) are:

$$_t - _{t-1} = -\frac{_{t-1}}{-U_{t-1}}(U_t - U_{t-1}) = \delta_U \quad (4.1)$$

$$_t - _{t-1} = -\frac{_{t-1}}{-U_{t-1}}(U_t - U_{t-1}) = \delta_U \quad (4.2)$$

$$_t = _{t-1} - ([U_t - U_{t-1}] + \delta_U + \delta_U) \quad (4.3)$$

where
Total area, $A = U_t + C_t + F_t + P_t$.

## Rent-Biased Urbanization Model

For this model, we continue to assume that urbanization exclusively determines changes in rural land uses. However, in this model we allow the rents accruing to different rural land uses to influence these changes—i.e., to allow for disproportional change among rural uses.

This is a simple extension of the Rent Neutral Urbanization Model where we allow the relative values of crop and forest uses to influence the effects of urbanization on rural land. Equations 4.1–6.1 are modified to allow the change in rural uses to be affected by forest and crop rent proxies.

$$_t = _{t-1} + \left[\alpha_c + \beta_{cc}p_c + \beta_c p\right]\delta_U \quad (5.1)$$
$$(-) \quad (+) \quad (-)$$

$$_t = _{t-1} + \left[\alpha + \beta_c p_c + \beta p\right]\delta_U \quad (5.2)$$
$$(-) \quad (-) \quad (+)$$

$$_t = _{t-1} - ([U_t - U_{t-1}] + [_t - _{t-1}] + [_t - _{t-1}]) \quad (5.3)$$

where:
$\delta$'s are defined by equations 4.1 and 4.2

$p_c$ and $p_f$ = variables that proxy for rents accruing to crop and forest uses respectively

$\beta$'s = estimated coefficients with the expected signs indicated (e.g., we expect the crop rent coefficient to be positive in equation 5.1 because higher prices would reduce the loss of cropland to urban uses).

The Rent-Biased Urbanization and Rural Substitution models were only applied to eastern regions and rangeland uses were held constant—i.e., the mutable land base is restricted to urban, cropland, forest, and pasture uses.

## Rural Substitution Model

A third formulation allows for rural land uses to change in response to changes in rural land rent determinants in addition to urbanization. Changes to relative rents could lead to rural land use switching irrespective of population/income changes. Consider the equations for current amounts of forest and cropland uses similar to equation (2):

$$_t = \varphi + \varphi\,p_t + \varphi_c\,p_{ct} + \varphi\,U_t + \delta^- + \alpha^- + \varepsilon_U \quad (6.1)$$

$$_t = \gamma + \gamma_c\,p_t + \gamma_{cc}\,p_{ct} + \gamma_c\,U_t + \delta_c^- + \alpha_c^- + \varepsilon_U \quad (6.2)$$

Here we assume that the areas of land in forest and cropland are determined by the time-varying rents accruing to wood products and crops ($p$'s) and vectors of observed and unobserved fixed attributes that influence the suitability of land for various uses ($Z$ and $Y$ respectively). Pasture area ($P$) is defined as a residual land use. Rental values for forest and crop uses and the area of urban use are considered time-varying. To account for the urbanization dynamic in the Rent-Biased Urbanization Model, we substitute equations (5.1) and (5.2) for urban change terms in equations (7.1) and (7.2) as follows:

$$_t = _{t-1} + \left[\alpha_c + \beta_{cc}\,_{ct} + \beta_c\,_t\right]\delta_c + \varphi_c\left[_t - _{t-1}\right] + \varphi_{cc}\left[_{ct} - _{ct-1}\right] + \varepsilon^* \quad (7.1)$$

$$_t = {}_{t-1} + \left[\alpha + \beta_c {}_{ct} + \beta {}_t\right]\delta +$$

$$\gamma_c \left[{}_{ct} - {}_{ct-1}\right] + \gamma \left[{}_t - {}_{t-1}\right] + \varepsilon^* \quad (7.2)$$

$$_t = {}_{t-1} - \left([U_t - U_{t-1}] + \right.$$

$$\left. \cdot \left[{}_t - {}_{t-1}\right] + \left[{}_t - {}_{t-1}\right]\right) \quad (7.3)$$

For the Rent Neutral Urbanization Model, we estimated equation (3) using weighted least squares, weighted by the square root of the area of the county to account for non-constant variances. For the Rent-Biased Urbanization and Rural Substitution Models we applied a weighted Seemingly Unrelated Estimation approach to also account for cross equation correlations. The Rent-Biased Urbanization Model requires joint estimation of equations 3, 5.1, and 5.2 while the Rural Substitution Model requires estimation of

equations 3, 7.1, and 7.2. Coefficient estimates are described in Wear (2010).

**Forecasting Algorithm**

These models are designed to forecast change in the areas of urban, forest, and crop uses with pasture use as a residual. Because areas in any land use are not constrained to be positive by the structure of these equations, nonegativity constraints and "adding-up" rules need to be applied to ensure logical forecasts. For the forecasts developed for this report we adopted the rent neutral urbanization models for the North, Pacific, and Rocky Mountain Regions. Including rural rent variables in the models for these regions added little information to the forecasts. Models for the South showed strong improvements in explanatory power using the Rural Substitution model. This form of the model was applied to the South but forecasts described here hold the relative rents of the crop and forest land uses constant over time.

## Appendix B—Rural Land Use Complexity Index

We construct a complexity index as a gauge of the potential for land use change among rural land uses within a county. At one end of this spectrum are counties that are dominated by native land uses such as forest or range, where inherent productivity or economic demands preclude active agricultural management. At the other end of this spectrum are lands that are dominated by crops, where soil productivity and markets favor intensive agricultural production. Between these two extremes, intensive and extensive agricultural land uses coexist with native cover in varying quantities. We hypothesize that land use changes are more likely to occur in these middle zones where land use complexity ($LUC$) is high, because this is where returns to alternative uses are likely to be comparable and where small variations in relative returns could cause changes in land allocations among uses.

To construct a land use complexity index, we utilize a standard diversity formula from information theory. The entropy or complexity of a system (land within a county) with $n$ possible States (land uses) is defined as:

$$LUC = -k \sum_{i=1}^{n} p_i \ln p_i$$

where

$p_i$ = the observed proportion of land use i, the sum of these proportions is 1 (100 percent)

$k$ = a scaling parameter.

If a county has only one rural land use, then one of the $p_i$'s is equal to one and the logarithm of one is zero (we apply the rule that the logarithm of zero, in the limit, is equal to one), so the complexity index is equal to zero. The highest value of the $LUC$ is achieved where land uses are equal across all classes. This occurs where $p_i$ is equal to $1/n$—where no single land use represents a majority of the county. We define the scaling factor ($k$) equal to $1/[\sum_{i=1}^{n} 1/n \ln\{1/n\}] = 1/\ln\{1/n\}$ so that $LUC$ ranges from zero (least complex) to one (maximum complexity).

We implement the complexity index by defining the proportion of land use across three use classes: cropland, pasture, and native, defined as the sum of range and forests in the county so $n$ is equal to three. We further modify the definition of $LUC$ to account for the proportion of the county that is in a rural use ($R$) as follows:

$$LUC = -Rk \sum_{i=1}^{n} p_i \ln p_i$$

So the range of $LUC$ now depends on the availability of rural land. $LUC$ is at a maximum where all rural land uses occur in equal proportion and where the rural proportion of the county ($R$) is equal to one. $LUC$ is at a minimum either where one rural land use occurs ($p_i = 1$) or where there is no rural land ($R=0$).

# Appendix C —Data Tables

**Table C1Ñ Forecasts of land uses for Scenario A1B in the United States by region, 1997Ð2060**[a]

| Subregion | Year | Land use category | | | | | Total area |
|-----------|------|-------|----------|--------|---------|-------|------------|
| | | Urban | Cropland | Forest | Pasture | Range | |
| | | *thousand acres* | | | | | |
| North | | | | | | | |
| | 1997 | 28,929 | 142,190 | 149,747 | 36,063 | 86 | 357,015 |
| | 2010 | 33,445 | 140,183 | 147,763 | 35,538 | 86 | 357,015 |
| | 2020 | 37,590 | 138,350 | 145,928 | 35,060 | 86 | 357,015 |
| | 2030 | 41,316 | 136,706 | 144,267 | 34,640 | 86 | 357,015 |
| | 2040 | 45,488 | 134,857 | 142,413 | 34,171 | 86 | 357,015 |
| | 2050 | 50,172 | 132,771 | 140,338 | 33,648 | 86 | 357,015 |
| | 2060 | 55,441 | 130,417 | 138,007 | 33,064 | 86 | 357,015 |
| Pacific | | | | | | | |
| | 1997 | 6,997 | 19,770 | 38,433 | 4,115 | 32,983 | 102,298 |
| | 2010 | 8,736 | 19,414 | 37,736 | 4,030 | 32,382 | 102,298 |
| | 2020 | 9,880 | 19,182 | 37,262 | 3,975 | 31,999 | 102,298 |
| | 2030 | 10,958 | 18,962 | 36,813 | 3,923 | 31,642 | 102,298 |
| | 2040 | 12,109 | 18,727 | 36,331 | 3,870 | 31,261 | 102,298 |
| | 2050 | 13,339 | 18,476 | 35,818 | 3,814 | 30,850 | 102,298 |
| | 2060 | 14,662 | 18,206 | 35,267 | 3,756 | 30,406 | 102,298 |
| Rockies | | | | | | | |
| | 1997 | 6,851 | 123,385 | 28,744 | 15,596 | 256,332 | 430,907 |
| | 2010 | 9,138 | 122,728 | 28,484 | 15,467 | 255,091 | 430,907 |
| | 2020 | 10,694 | 122,267 | 28,302 | 15,382 | 254,261 | 430,907 |
| | 2030 | 12,154 | 121,845 | 28,127 | 15,303 | 253,477 | 430,907 |
| | 2040 | 13,727 | 121,386 | 27,952 | 15,218 | 252,623 | 430,907 |
| | 2050 | 15,475 | 120,874 | 27,761 | 15,128 | 251,669 | 430,907 |
| | 2060 | 17,375 | 120,299 | 27,556 | 15,032 | 250,645 | 430,907 |
| South | | | | | | | |
| | 1997 | 29,879 | 84,292 | 175,812 | 61,191 | 111,854 | 463,029 |
| | 2010 | 38,368 | 81,736 | 171,837 | 60,109 | 110,979 | 463,029 |
| | 2020 | 44,923 | 79,842 | 168,482 | 59,285 | 110,497 | 463,029 |
| | 2030 | 50,770 | 78,213 | 165,481 | 58,497 | 110,068 | 463,029 |
| | 2040 | 57,083 | 76,462 | 162,178 | 57,701 | 109,606 | 463,029 |
| | 2050 | 63,966 | 74,563 | 158,544 | 56,831 | 109,124 | 463,029 |
| | 2060 | 71,630 | 72,498 | 154,434 | 55,863 | 108,604 | 463,029 |
| Total | | | | | | | |
| | 1997 | 72,656 | 369,637 | 392,736 | 116,965 | 401,255 | 1,353,249 |
| | 2010 | 89,687 | 364,061 | 385,820 | 115,144 | 398,538 | 1,353,249 |
| | 2020 | 103,087 | 359,641 | 379,974 | 113,702 | 396,843 | 1,353,249 |
| | 2030 | 115,198 | 355,726 | 374,688 | 112,363 | 395,273 | 1,353,249 |
| | 2040 | 128,407 | 351,432 | 368,874 | 110,960 | 393,576 | 1,353,249 |
| | 2050 | 142,952 | 346,684 | 362,461 | 109,421 | 391,729 | 1,353,249 |
| | 2060 | 159,108 | 341,420 | 355,264 | 107,715 | 389,741 | 1,353,249 |

[a] Total area refers to the ÒmutableÓ area defined by the sum of nonfederal urban, cropland, pasture, and range uses.

**Table C2Ñ Forecasts of land uses for Scenario A2 in the United States by region, 1997Ð2060[a]**

| Subregion | Year | Land use category | | | | | Total area |
|---|---|---|---|---|---|---|---|
| | | Urban | Cropland | Forest | Pasture | Range | |
| | | *thousand acres* | | | | | |
| North | | | | | | | |
| | 1997 | 28,929 | 142,190 | 149,747 | 36,063 | 86 | 357,015 |
| | 2010 | 32,704 | 140,549 | 148,053 | 35,623 | 86 | 357,015 |
| | 2020 | 36,105 | 139,072 | 146,524 | 35,228 | 86 | 357,015 |
| | 2030 | 39,140 | 137,762 | 145,143 | 34,884 | 86 | 357,015 |
| | 2040 | 42,375 | 136,363 | 143,673 | 34,518 | 86 | 357,015 |
| | 2050 | 46,182 | 134,710 | 141,945 | 34,091 | 86 | 357,015 |
| | 2060 | 50,687 | 132,750 | 139,897 | 33,595 | 86 | 357,015 |
| Pacific | | | | | | | |
| | 1997 | 6,997 | 19,770 | 38,433 | 4,115 | 32,983 | 102,298 |
| | 2010 | 8,741 | 19,409 | 37,735 | 4,029 | 32,384 | 102,298 |
| | 2020 | 9,858 | 19,178 | 37,270 | 3,974 | 32,017 | 102,298 |
| | 2030 | 10,930 | 18,955 | 36,821 | 3,923 | 31,669 | 102,298 |
| | 2040 | 12,081 | 18,715 | 36,336 | 3,869 | 31,297 | 102,298 |
| | 2050 | 13,397 | 18,440 | 35,782 | 3,809 | 30,870 | 102,298 |
| | 2060 | 14,928 | 18,119 | 35,137 | 3,742 | 30,372 | 102,298 |
| Rockies | | | | | | | |
| | 1997 | 6,851 | 123,385 | 28,744 | 15,596 | 256,332 | 430,907 |
| | 2010 | 8,981 | 122,805 | 28,491 | 15,476 | 255,155 | 430,907 |
| | 2020 | 10,383 | 122,419 | 28,316 | 15,400 | 254,388 | 430,907 |
| | 2030 | 11,706 | 122,071 | 28,149 | 15,329 | 253,652 | 430,907 |
| | 2040 | 13,107 | 121,709 | 27,981 | 15,254 | 252,856 | 430,907 |
| | 2050 | 14,644 | 121,297 | 27,798 | 15,177 | 251,991 | 430,907 |
| | 2060 | 16,500 | 120,802 | 27,578 | 15,085 | 250,942 | 430,907 |
| South | | | | | | | |
| | 1997 | 29,879 | 84,292 | 175,812 | 61,191 | 111,854 | 463,029 |
| | 2010 | 37,852 | 81,753 | 172,413 | 60,489 | 110,993 | 463,029 |
| | 2020 | 43,710 | 79,989 | 169,675 | 59,576 | 110,549 | 463,029 |
| | 2030 | 48,709 | 78,651 | 167,252 | 58,748 | 110,140 | 463,029 |
| | 2040 | 53,837 | 77,287 | 164,747 | 57,913 | 109,716 | 463,029 |
| | 2050 | 59,699 | 75,747 | 161,861 | 56,953 | 109,240 | 463,029 |
| | 2060 | 66,452 | 73,975 | 158,498 | 55,889 | 108,686 | 463,029 |
| Total | | | | | | | |
| | 1997 | 72,656 | 369,637 | 392,736 | 116,965 | 401,255 | 1,353,249 |
| | 2010 | 88,278 | 364,516 | 386,692 | 115,617 | 398,618 | 1,353,249 |
| | 2020 | 100,056 | 360,658 | 381,785 | 114,178 | 397,040 | 1,353,249 |
| | 2030 | 110,485 | 357,439 | 377,365 | 112,884 | 395,547 | 1,353,249 |
| | 2040 | 121,400 | 354,074 | 372,737 | 111,554 | 393,955 | 1,353,249 |
| | 2050 | 133,922 | 350,194 | 367,386 | 110,030 | 392,187 | 1,353,249 |
| | 2060 | 148,567 | 345,646 | 361,110 | 108,311 | 390,086 | 1,353,249 |

[a]Total area refers to the ÒmutableÓ area defined by the sum of nonfederal urban, cropland, pasture, and range uses.

**Table C3Ñ Forecasts of land uses for Scenario B2 in the United States by region, 1997Ð2060[a]**

| Subregion | Year | Land use category | | | | | Total area |
|-----------|------|-------|----------|--------|---------|-------|------------|
| | | Urban | Cropland | Forest | Pasture | Range | |
| | | *thousand acres* | | | | | |
| North | | | | | | | |
| | 1997 | 28,929 | 142,190 | 149,747 | 36,063 | 86 | 357,015 |
| | 2010 | 34,555 | 139,669 | 147,290 | 35,416 | 86 | 357,015 |
| | 2020 | 37,662 | 138,310 | 145,906 | 35,051 | 86 | 357,015 |
| | 2030 | 39,237 | 137,630 | 145,199 | 34,863 | 86 | 357,015 |
| | 2040 | 41,135 | 136,789 | 144,367 | 34,638 | 86 | 357,015 |
| | 2050 | 43,695 | 135,652 | 143,238 | 34,344 | 86 | 357,015 |
| | 2060 | 45,437 | 134,901 | 142,450 | 34,142 | 86 | 357,015 |
| Pacific | | | | | | | |
| | 1997 | 6,997 | 19,770 | 38,433 | 4,115 | 32,983 | 102,298 |
| | 2010 | 8,859 | 19,393 | 37,687 | 4,025 | 32,334 | 102,298 |
| | 2020 | 9,860 | 19,186 | 37,270 | 3,976 | 32,006 | 102,298 |
| | 2030 | 10,528 | 19,045 | 36,985 | 3,942 | 31,797 | 102,298 |
| | 2040 | 11,158 | 18,913 | 36,716 | 3,911 | 31,601 | 102,298 |
| | 2050 | 11,911 | 18,755 | 36,397 | 3,876 | 31,359 | 102,298 |
| | 2060 | 12,590 | 18,608 | 36,108 | 3,844 | 31,147 | 102,298 |
| Rockies | | | | | | | |
| | 1997 | 6,851 | 123,385 | 28,744 | 15,596 | 256,332 | 430,907 |
| | 2010 | 9,411 | 122,617 | 28,462 | 15,451 | 254,966 | 430,907 |
| | 2020 | 10,699 | 122,260 | 28,304 | 15,382 | 254,263 | 430,907 |
| | 2030 | 11,536 | 122,060 | 28,192 | 15,337 | 253,783 | 430,907 |
| | 2040 | 12,424 | 121,828 | 28,084 | 15,291 | 253,281 | 430,907 |
| | 2050 | 13,512 | 121,529 | 27,960 | 15,235 | 252,671 | 430,907 |
| | 2060 | 14,438 | 121,312 | 27,846 | 15,190 | 252,121 | 430,907 |
| South | | | | | | | |
| | 1997 | 29,879 | 84,292 | 175,812 | 61,191 | 111,854 | 463,029 |
| | 2010 | 40,288 | 80,986 | 170,996 | 60,315 | 110,915 | 463,029 |
| | 2020 | 45,768 | 79,338 | 168,435 | 59,459 | 110,499 | 463,029 |
| | 2030 | 48,739 | 78,604 | 167,025 | 58,892 | 110,242 | 463,029 |
| | 2040 | 52,043 | 77,754 | 165,351 | 58,365 | 109,987 | 463,029 |
| | 2050 | 56,234 | 76,644 | 163,196 | 57,743 | 109,683 | 463,029 |
| | 2060 | 59,318 | 75,864 | 161,660 | 57,232 | 109,426 | 463,029 |
| Total | | | | | | | |
| | 1997 | 72,656 | 369,637 | 392,736 | 116,965 | 401,255 | 1,353,249 |
| | 2010 | 93,113 | 362,665 | 384,435 | 115,207 | 398,301 | 1,353,249 |
| | 2020 | 103,989 | 359,094 | 379,915 | 113,868 | 396,854 | 1,353,249 |
| | 2030 | 110,040 | 357,339 | 377,401 | 113,034 | 395,908 | 1,353,249 |
| | 2040 | 116,760 | 355,284 | 374,518 | 112,205 | 394,955 | 1,353,249 |
| | 2050 | 125,352 | 352,580 | 370,791 | 111,198 | 393,799 | 1,353,249 |
| | 2060 | 131,783 | 350,685 | 368,064 | 110,408 | 392,780 | 1,353,249 |

[a]Total area refers to the ÒmutableÓ area defined by the sum of nonfederal urban, cropland, pasture, and range uses.

www.ingramcontent.com/pod-product-compliance
Lightning Source LLC
Chambersburg PA
CBHW081123280526
45787CB00007B/2960